# Getting Started

You may already have some wool—maybe you are raising a few sheep yourself, or you know someone who is. If you are lucky enough to have a fleece already, great! You can start off with that. You can try spinning "in the grease" if you want, meaning you'll spin the wool without washing it. But I think you'll find spinning washed or "scoured" wool easier and nicer (see Scouring (Washing) Your Wool, page 21). So I recommend that you wash up some wool, and then you're ready to begin.

If you don't have a source of washed or greasy wool, there are several places to try. You can search the internet easily using a search engine, try in the advertisements in *Spin-Off* magazine (a colorful quarterly magazine for handspinners published by Interweave Press), or your local phone directory under "Weaving," "Knitting," or "Yarn" for shops with spinning supplies in your area.

*Spin-Off* magazine maintains a directory of spinning guilds on their website, www.interweave.com/spin/ or ask your spinning and weaving supplier about local spinning guilds. The guild members will not only be able to help you find a fleece (or part of one), they will undoubtedly love to have you join the guild and will offer spinning help.

Spinning and weaving shops usually carry several publications related to spinning, in which you will find many ads for fiber (see Resources, page 33).

You can get a "spinning kit," containing one or more types of wool and a handspindle for experimenting from several sources. These will be adequate for getting started. Again, look in the advertisements in the resources listed above.

## BEGINNING TO SPIN

Now that you've got a bit of wool, the only other tools you'll need to get started are your two hands. Begin with a small handful of wool. Gently and gradually separate the fibers from one another so that they are uniformly open and relatively untangled. The object is to separate the fibers from one another so that each one freely slips past its neighbors when you need it to. Once your fibers are teased open, you are ready to spin.

Now hold the mass of fibers gently and loosely in one hand. With the other hand, pinch a small group of fibers (ten to twenty or so) and begin to pull them out from the fiber mass, about an inch and a half. Don't pull so hard or so far that you separate these fibers from the rest of the fiber mass—you want to be able to manipulate their front ends just now, but you want their hind ends to stay buried in the mass of wool (the **fiber supply**). What you have just done is called **drafting** fibers, in preparation for **twisting** them into yarn.

Lay the extended fiber ends against your thigh. Hold them all together beneath your right forefinger. Now twist the fibers by rolling them against your right leg as you rub your finger toward your knee. You'll see the drafted fibers twist together, and the twist will begin to run up your newly made yarn toward the fiber supply. When the twist just reaches the fiber supply, pick the yarn end up—be careful not to let the twist unwind—and bring it back toward your hip for the next roll down your leg.

Before you roll it again, though, gently pull out an additional inch or two of fibers: Just give an easy tug on the beginning of the yarn. Be sure to hold the fiber supply with a light touch so that the fibers can slip as you need them to; you don't want to be playing tug-of-war on either end of the same fibers. If you watch closely, you'll see some of the twist that you've put in your yarn begin to run into the newly drafted fibers. Now, just as before, hold the beginning end of the yarn under your forefinger and roll it down your leg.

Teasing wool makes it open and fluffy, so it's easier to spin. The left hand here holds a small clump of unteased fibers. The right hand lightly plucks at the fibers to loosen them.

When you are ready to spin, pinch a small group of fibers and begin to pull them out from the fiber mass.

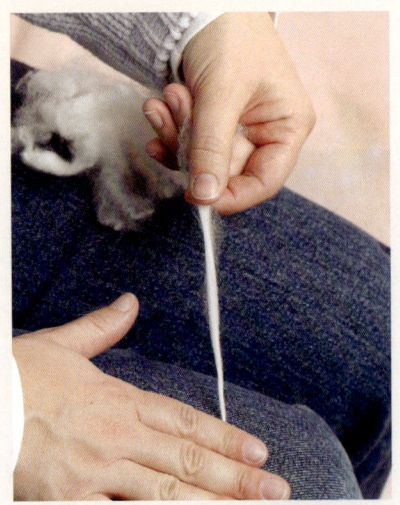

As you roll your finger across the fibers, they will twist together. The twist will run up the extended fibers toward the fiber supply.

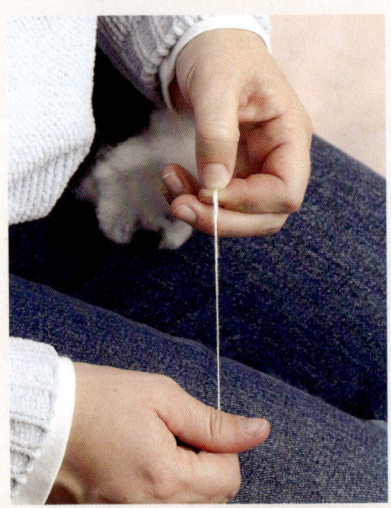

After you make a length of yarn, test its strength by holding both ends and pulling gently.

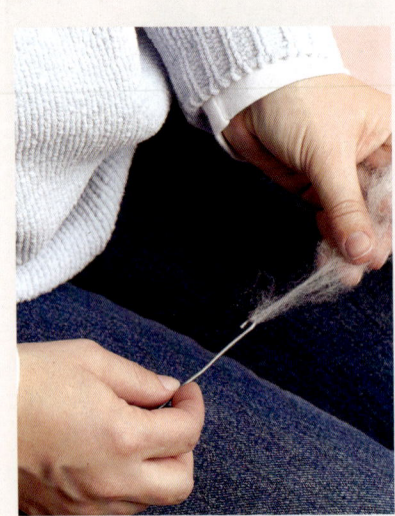

To begin spinning with the hooked stick, pick up a small group of fibers at the edge of the fiber supply and gently pull this group away from the mass.

*You have just made yarn!* You have performed the two basic actions required of spinning: **drafting** and **twisting** fibers.

Continue as you were doing before, keeping the yarn tight as you draft and then roll. In that way, the twist can move, or "travel," along the length of the yarn, evening itself out instead of building up in one place. Be sure you always twist in the same direction, and that you keep the twisted end from undoing itself.

As you continue, you'll see the yarn growing and your two hands moving farther and farther apart: the beginning end of the yarn in one hand, the fiber supply in the other. Here's a simple test that will tell you if your yarn is good and strong: Keep hold of the beginning end and, with your other hand, pinch the yarn just in front of the fiber supply. Now steadily, but gently, try to pull the two ends farther apart. If you feel your hands moving apart, even a little bit, the fibers are slipping past one another. That means the yarn isn't twisted quite enough to hold the fibers together. Here is your **first rule of spinning:** *If you don't twist the drafted fibers enough, your yarn will drift apart and break.* The remedy? Twist the fibers some more without doing any more drafting, and then test the yarn again. When you can tug gently on both ends of the yarn and nothing happens, you know that you have enough twist in your yarn to make it strong.

If you are really good at rolling the yarn end down your leg, you may find that your little length of yarn is twisted so much that drafting more fibers becomes difficult. Which brings us to the **second rule of spinning:** *If you twist the drafted fibers too much, the twist will travel into the fiber supply, engulfing it and preventing further drafting.* You can fix this mistake by gradually untwisting the yarn (not the fiber supply) until you can draft again.

So, yes, there are such things as too little and too much twist, but there is a lot of leeway in between and there will always be tests that you can do to judge the right amount of twist for your yarn. For now, if you can keep drafting and twisting bit by bit, and your yarn is holding together, you're doing great.

But what are you going to do with that length of yarn stretched between your hands? How can you secure or store what you have made so that it will not untwist, and so that you can keep adding to its length? One of the first solutions that the ancients came up with was the "hooked stick," a tool still in use today.

## Spinning on the Hooked Stick

You can make your own hooked stick by cutting yourself a twelve-inch length of wire coat hanger. Sand the cut ends smooth so that there are no sharp burrs to catch on your hands or on the wool. With some needle-nose pliers, bend one end into a shepherd's crook. Bend the hook back a bit so that the topmost curve of the bend is in direct line with the shaft, as shown. This bend will keep vibrations out of your yarn as you are twisting the stick.

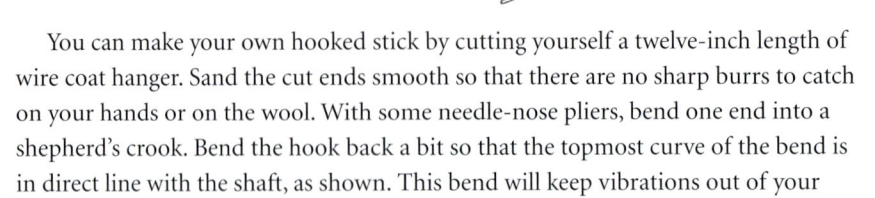

Here's how to start spinning on the hooked stick if you don't already have a length of finger-spun yarn. Take a small handful of wool fiber and tease it gently apart into a uniform mass, as before. With your stick, hook a small group of fibers near the edge of the fiber supply. Holding the shaft of the stick, gently pull out those hooked fibers an inch or two from the fiber supply. Now put the shaft of the stick down on your leg and roll it slowly from your knee to your hip with your fingers and palm. This is a much more efficient way to twist fibers, isn't it? Very rapidly the twist will enter the yarn and move up to the fiber supply—and that's as far as you want it to go.

Just as before, pick up the stick and move it back toward your knee in preparation for the next roll. Draft an additional length of fibers, about two inches, then roll the shaft up your leg. Always keep the yarn tight so that the twist will distribute itself evenly along the length of the yarn, and so the yarn won't collapse and twist on itself. Keep a constant hold on both the fiber supply and the stick, or your yarn may untwist. (You still haven't reached the stage where you can store your yarn.) Continue drafting and twisting until you have a couple of feet of yarn.

## Winding On

Once you have spun a length of yarn, you will be ready to store that portion on the stick so that you can continue. Before you store it, be sure to test the yarn for sufficient twist by giving it a gentle tug between your hands. If it doesn't drift apart, it's ready to be wound on. If it does drift apart, then add more twist before winding on.

Keeping the yarn tight, slip the loop of fibers down from the top of the hook to the middle of the shaft. Hold the loop firmly in place on the middle of the shaft. As you begin turning the stick in your hand, wind the yarn around the shaft. Hold the fiber supply stationary, and the yarn taut, while you turn the stick in the *same direction* that you used to twist your yarn. The yarn should be wound in the center of the shaft, and it should be wound firmly (so it doesn't slip around the shaft) in small overlapping turns (to keep it compact). Stop when you have about an eight-inch length of yarn left. Now keep turning the stick in the same direction, but begin to spiral the yarn up the shaft toward the hook in a barber pole pattern. The last wrap should be made directly under the hook. You should have a few inches of yarn extending out from the hook to form the anchor for your next length of yarn. You are ready to begin again. Go at your own pace, spinning and winding on a few more lengths of yarn.

## The Drafting Zone

When you've spun a bit more, hold a length of yarn and the fiber supply out in front of you. Note the small triangular area *between* the yarn and the fiber supply. It's called the **drafting triangle** or the **drafting zone**. It is a transition area where the drafted fibers meet the twist. *That is where yarn is made.* In any kind of spinning, it deserves your constant attention. The size, consistency, texture, and character of your yarn are determined in that little space. Watch how the size and shape of the drafting zone change as you work. Drafting new fibers elongates the triangle, and adding twist shortens it; drafting a greater number of fibers thickens the triangle (your yarn becomes thicker as well), and drafting fewer fibers thins it.

## Problems

Are you running into any problems? Does the drafting seem difficult? Here's an explanation of some common problems.

*Too much twist.* You may be adding too much twist for the number and length of fibers you've drafted. If so, try this remedy: As you slowly roll the stick up your leg, watch the twist as it travels up the fibers you have drafted. Stop adding twist as it reaches the end of the drafted fibers, just before it starts to enter the fiber supply itself. Once the twist enters the fiber supply, it will try to engulf the whole mass into a gigantic super-yarn. Friction will then hold all the twisted fibers together and make drafting just a portion of them difficult or impossible.

*Insufficient teasing.* If too much twist doesn't seem to be the problem, it may be that your fiber supply isn't teased enough. Remember that the fibers must be completely free to slip past one another. Loose, open fibers draft easily.

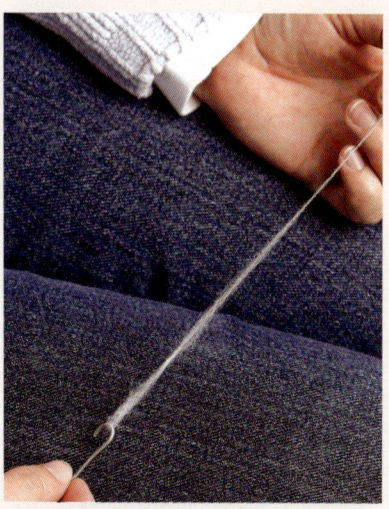

Once again, make sure you have enough twist in your yarn. This piece wasn't twisted enough—it's drifting apart and is about to break.

Wind your yarn onto the center of the hooked stick in the same direction you used to spin your yarn.

Make your last warp directly under the hook and you're ready to spin again.

*Too much tension*. Another common problem is holding the fibers too tightly for them to slip past your fingers and into the yarn. First relax your fingers; then relax all the muscles clear up into your shoulder. Spinning should be restful, and you'll have a much easier time of it if you remind yourself to keep everything loose. Your hand holding the fibers may be too close to the drafting zone. With the twist firmly holding one end of the fibers, and your fingers firmly holding the other end of the very same fibers, what you have is a tug-of-war, not drafting. Hold the fiber supply delicately, several inches back from the drafting zone.

*Insufficient twist*. Does the yarn just slip apart when you try to draft, instead of pulling along new fibers out of the supply? Then you need more twist to hold the yarn together. Make sure the twist travels all the way up to the edge of the main fiber supply before you draft more fibers. The compressing friction of the twist has to move up and grasp a few more fiber ends so that they will be pulled along into the next drafted section. Be sure you're holding the fiber supply loosely so that you're not accidentally preventing the fibers from moving into the yarn.

A slub

*Lumpy yarn*. What about all those lumps (also called **slubs**) in the yarn? For heaven's sake, don't worry about smoothness yet—that will come with practice. Lumps happen for a variety of reasons, but basically they form because the same number of fibers did not continuously pass through the drafting zone at a constant speed, proportionate with the advancing twist. The fat places are where too many fibers came through as a bunch, and the thin places are where too few came through. And remember, sometimes it's all in the way you look at it. Some spinners who want novelty effects appreciate the thick-and-thin look as a design element.

We talked about keeping the yarn tight so that twist would not build up in one place, but would travel the length of the yarn and even itself out. It's important for you to note, however, what happens to the twist when the yarn is unevenly spun. Take a look at the fat places in your yarn. The twist won't travel through them, even when the yarn is held taut. Instead, it builds up in the thin sections. This is a property of yarn structure, and you'll find it to be true no matter what fiber you are spinning. Given that property, there is something to be said for keeping your yarns reasonably even. When they are, their strength and abrasion resistance is not only more uniform throughout the length of the yarn, it is actually higher overall. But for now, your aim is just to make a sound yarn: one that doesn't pull apart, and one that doesn't twist up on itself uncontrollably.

Do you have a particularly large lump that you would really like to get rid of? Here's a trick of the trade for you. Take hold of the yarn on either side of the offending lump, about an inch or so away from where it thickens. Turn your hands in opposite directions so that the yarn between them begins to untwist, just to the point where you can feel it begin to drift apart. Gently stretch the lump (the fibers in the lump will begin to slide past one another) until it is the size you want. Let the yarn go and watch the twist run into the newly stretched portion. (If you can't get the lump to start drifting, your hands are too close together. Move them slightly farther apart and try again.)

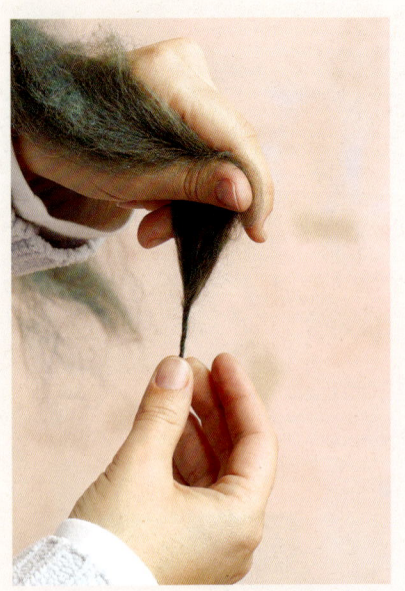

The drafting zone is the triangle area where yarn is made. If the twist enters the fiber supply, you will find it difficult or impossible to draft. Keep the twist out of the drafting zone.

The **length** of the drafting zone will depend on the length of the fibers you are spinning. If you are having trouble getting the fibers to draft, your hand may be too close to the fiber supply. Move your hand back from the drafting zone.

## DRAFTING AND TWISTING SIMULTANEOUSLY

When you begin to feel comfortable with drafting and twisting in sequence, try combining the two steps. As you slowly add twist by rolling the stick down your leg, draft the fibers by pulling back gently on the fiber supply and letting some fibers slip through. Be sure to keep an eye on the twist and how it travels. You'll need to add twist at the same rate that you draft fibers, letting neither process get ahead of the other. The twist should consistently enter the drafted fibers just an inch or so in front of the fiber supply. Try spinning a short length of yarn this way and then test it for soundness.

As you continue to draft and twist simultaneously, pay constant attention to the drafting zone. Ideally, a spinner wants to keep the same number of fibers entering the zone at one end while the twist enters the fibers at the same point on the other end. If the drafting triangle gets long, then the twisting rate is falling behind the drafting rate. If the triangle gets short, then the twisting rate is faster than the drafting rate. See how close you can come to keeping the drafting triangle constant in size and shape, and notice what happens to your yarn as that zone varies.

There is a relationship between the size of the yarn you want to make and the amount of twist required to hold it together. Here's the **third rule of spinning** for you: *The fewer the number of fibers that you draft and the finer the diameter of the yarn, the more twist you will need to hold it together.* On the other hand, the more fibers and the thicker the yarn, the less twist you will need to bind the fibers together. Test this rule for yourself, spinning thin and thick yarns, checking them for soundness, and watching how they change as you use more or less twist.

## DIRECTION OF TWIST—Z AND S

Yarn can be twisted either clockwise (right) or counterclockwise (left). Think of the beginning of your yarn, the point where you first begin to twist it, as rotating in one or the other direction. The hook, which holds the beginning of your yarn on its shaft, can turn clockwise to give you what is called a "Z-twist" yarn. Or it can turn counterclockwise to give you what is called an "S-twist" yarn. No matter what tool twists the yarn—your hand, a stick, a spindle, or a spinning wheel—the direction in which the beginning rotates determines twist direction.

If you take a look at the drawings here, you'll see that the Z-twist yarn is so named because the fibers slant in the same direction as the downward stroke of the letter Z. Twisting your tool to the right gives you this result. Twisting it to the left makes an S-twist yarn, with the fibers slanting in the same direction as the downward stroke of the letter S.

Take a look at your own yarn. S or Z? Which way did the beginning rotate? If you held the fiber supply in your left hand and rolled the stick down your right leg (toward your knee), then your yarn is S-twisted, because the hook rolled counter-clockwise. If you held the fibers in your right hand and rolled the stick down your left leg, your yarn is Z-twisted.

Now here's an interesting experiment and an important point to remember. Turn this book upside down and take another look at the Z- and S-twist yarn sketches. No matter which way you look at them, upside down or right side up, a Z-twisted yarn is always a Z-twisted yarn, and an S-twisted yarn is always an S-twisted yarn. Check your yarn to see. Whether you started out with a Z- or an S-twist, that twist will remain in your yarn.

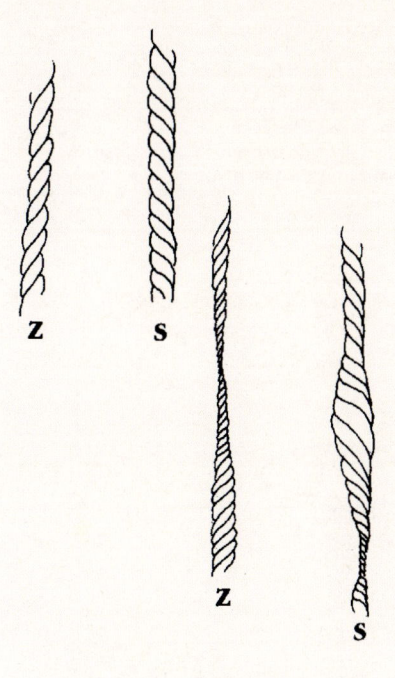

S is S, and Z is Z, whether right side up or upside down.

Fewer fibers? You'll need more twist. Lots of fibers? A smaller amount of twist will hold the yarn together.

The handspindle, which you can make yourself, is an ancient tool that is still being used today.

Top whorl spindle

Turkish handspindle

Spindle with painted whorl

If your spindle has no hook, secure the end of your thread with a half-hitch knot.

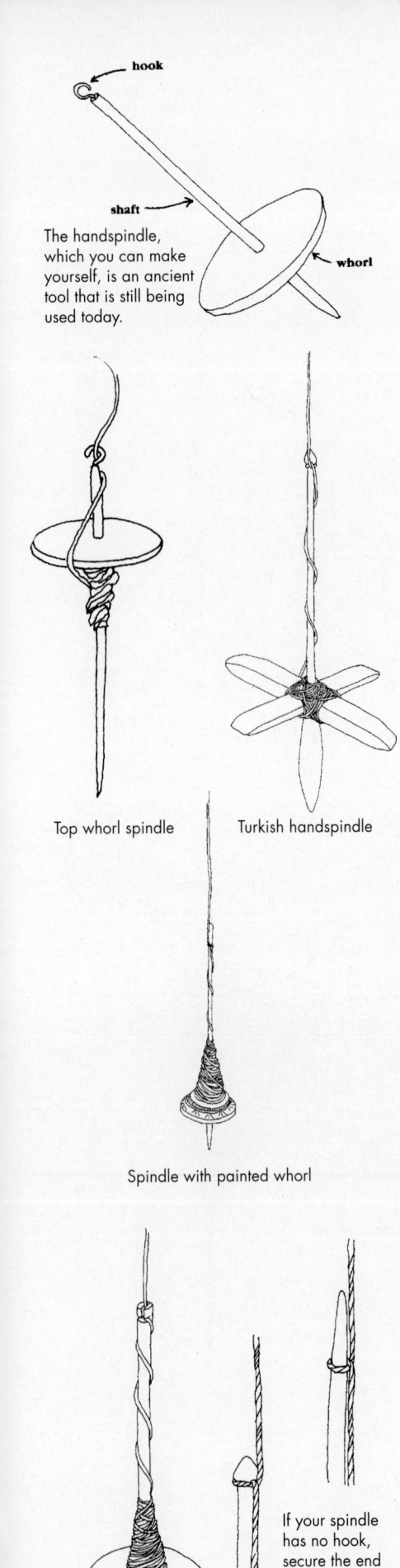

That's good to know for a couple of reasons. First, when you get into **plying** (twisting two or more yarns together), you'll need to know in which direction your original yarns were spun. But it won't matter if you mix up the starting or finishing ends. Once a Z, always a Z. And later on, once you start using your handspun in knitting, crocheting, and weaving, you'll find that Z- and S-twist yarns act a bit differently in certain situations. But no matter what convolutions you put yarn through in making your fabric, the twist directions will always remain the same.

Most of today's spinners tend to spin most of their singles yarns (as opposed to plied yarns) in the Z direction. Realize, however, that essentially there is no difference in a Z- or an S-twist yarn—they both do the job equally well—and you are free to spin in whatever direction pleases you. It's a good idea to be consistent in the direction you choose so that you don't have to spend a lot of time examining your yarns when you pick them up later for use in a plied yarn.

## Speeding It Up: Using the Handspindle

Handspindles have been used for countless generations, and can be found in use throughout the world to this day. In some countries they are used exclusively because their small size makes them easy to carry around. Yarn can be spun throughout the day between other activities, so yarn production is high.

The handspindle is a simple extension of the hooked stick concept. You just add a small weight to increase momentum, stand the stick upright, give it a good spin, and you can spin more yarn much faster. Most spindles consist of a wooden shaft with a small weight attached near one end. Shafts can be anywhere from eight to thirty-six inches long, but the most common is around twelve to fifteen inches. Many are tapered to a dull point near the weight at one end, with a carved or an attached hook at the other end. Others are gradually tapered at both ends. The weight, called a **whorl**, is a disk or ball of wood, stone, or clay with a hole in the middle. The whorl is slipped onto the end of the spindle shaft and is usually held in place by friction.

You can buy a variety of modern handspindles at spinning and weaving shops, or through the mail (see Resources, page 33), or you can make your own. Either way, there are a few things to keep in mind. The shaft should be straight and smooth—you want it to rotate smoothly and not to have rough places that will catch on your yarn. Although some spindles end in just a smooth taper at each end, you can spin more efficiently if there is a hook. Spindles with the hook at the same end as the whorl are called top whorl or high whorl spindles, and you can spin even faster with them. The whorl on all spindles should be round and evenly balanced, so that when the spindle is turning, it won't wobble and lose speed too quickly.

### HANDSPINDLE SPINNING

For consistency's sake, and to make the following instructions easier, spin your yarns with a Z-twist, turning the spindle in a clockwise direction. I suggest that you use your right hand to turn the spindle and your left to hold the fibers.

Just as you did with the hooked stick, hook a small group of fibers near the edge of the fiber supply. Holding the shaft of the handspindle in your right hand, gently pull out those hooked fibers an inch or two from the fiber supply. Now put the shaft of the spindle down on your leg and roll it slowly toward your hip with your fingers and palm. Once you've spun a length, unhook the yarn from the hook and, holding the yarn stationary against the shaft, rotate the spindle clockwise to firmly wrap the yarn around the shaft four or five times. The wrapping secures it. Then begin spiraling the yarn up the shaft in a barber pole pattern, just as you did with the hooked stick. Wrap the yarn fairly close, an inch or less apart, for a better grip on the shaft. Leave several inches of yarn extending beyond the end of the hook. If you are using a top whorl, wrap the yarn couple of times around the shaft to secure it, then take it over the whorl to the hook.

In the case of a handspindle that has no hook or notch at the top, a half-hitch knot is needed. After spiraling the yarn up the shaft, make a half hitch knot to secure the yarn before you spin.

## Make Your Own Handspindle

MATERIALS:

2 recycled compact disks (CDs)
1 3/8-inch diameter dowel (12 inches long)
1 eye hook (3/4 inches long)
1 rubber grommet with an inside diameter of 5/8 inch[1]

TOOLS:

Drill and drill bit slightly smaller than the eye hook
Safety goggles
Needle-nose pliers (with no teeth)
Vise clamp
Pencil
Sandpaper
Permanent ink marker

You can make a simple spindle using recycled compact disks, a grommet, a small eye hook, and a dowel.

Sand the ends of the dowel so they are smooth and have no burrs. On one end of the dowel rod, find the center and mark it with a pencil. Wearing safety goggles, secure the dowel in a vise clamp and drill a starter hole for the eye hook in the center. Screw in the eye hook, then open it with the needle-nose pliers so that it creates a hook.

With the marker, draw a clockwise arrow on the top CD. Place the two CDs together and insert the grommet through the center hole of the CDs so that the CDs rest inside the groove. Insert the dowel through the grommet and position the CDs about 2 inches down from the hook for a top whorl spindle or 10 inches down for a bottom whorl spindle.

Test your spindle for smooth rotation and balance by placing the end with the hook on the table and giving the top of the shaft a hearty spin. Keep it upright by loosely enclosing the top of the shaft with a circle of your fingers and thumb; allow it to spin freely. You'll need a bit of practice to get the hang of turning the spindle efficiently. If it turns smoothly like a top, you're in business. A little wobble is fine, but if your spindle wobbles a lot and slows down quickly, make another spindle. You'll enjoy spinning more with a spindle that works well.

[1] Grommets available from Bonkers Handmade Originals, PO Box 442099, Lawrence, KS 66044, www.bonkersfiber.com.

A CD spindle nestled in a basket full of Bonkers Handmade Originals dyed tops

1. Let the spindle hang down and give it a good twist in a clockwise direction with your right hand. After twist has built up, stop the spindle and hold it between your knees.

2. Put your right hand where your left hand is pinching the yarn and begin drafting the fiber with your left hand.

3. You'll find that drafting is easier if you draft new fibers just **before** the twist has reached the fiber supply—keep the fibers flowing very loosely.

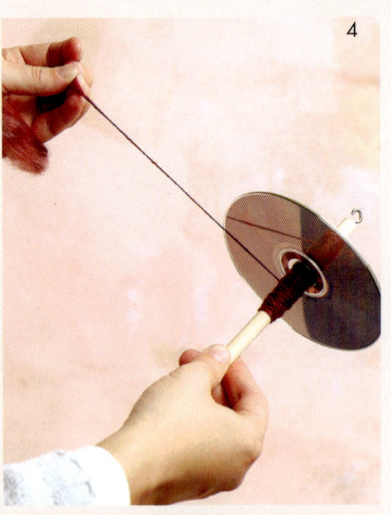

4. When you stand up to use the spindle, you'll be able to spin a greater length of yarn before you need to wind on.

5. At some point your yarn will break—then it is time to make a join.

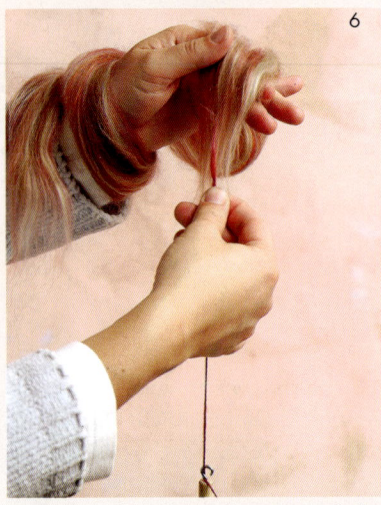

6. Make a good join by overlapping two fluffs of fiber and drafting them together.

## Getting Started

One of the best ways to start using a handspindle is to break down the actions of spinning the spindle and drafting. While sitting, pinch the yarn with your left hand just in front of the fiber supply so that the twist won't travel into it. Let the spindle hang down and give it a good twist in a clockwise direction with your right hand. After twist has built up, stop the spindle and hold it between your knees. Put your right hand where your left hand is pinching the yarn and begin drafting the fiber with your left hand. You'll find that drafting is easier if you draft new fibers just *before* the twist has reached the fiber supply—keep the fibers flowing very loosely. It also helps if you untwist the yarn a little with your right hand. Untwist the yarn by pinching it underneath the point where it becomes yarn, and unrolling the yarn about one inch down your index finger. The untwisted fibers will draft apart more easily. You can always add extra twist later to ensure a sound yarn. As you work, watch the drafting zone and try for a smooth flow of fibers meeting the advancing twist. Don't expect to be spinning perfect yarn here—none of us did at this stage! Just work for better and better control with your fingers as you practice. By working this way you can concentrate on drafting and controlling the twist without worrying about what the spindle is doing. Wind on the yarn you spun when you are ready for more twist.

## Winding On

To wind on your yarn, hold it taut while you turn the spindle shaft counterclockwise, unwinding the yarn spiraled around the shaft. (Did you remember to test it for the right amount of twist?) When you get to the end of the spirals, reverse direction again and begin winding on what you have just spun. Wind it all near the bottom of the shaft at the whorl. When you have about fifteen inches or so of yarn left, begin to spiral the yarn up the shaft and under the hook, leaving a few inches extending beyond the spindle tip to start your next length on a top whorl spindle, simply unhook the yarn and take it back over the whorl to wind on. Draft a bit of fiber, spin the spindle, and off you go again.

As you wind on more lengths of your handspun yarn, build up a cone shape of the yarn on the spindle. The widest part of the cone should be sitting next to the whorl. Keep the cone wide and short to encourage the weight of the yarn to stay as close to the whorl as possible. This positioning helps to increase your spinning momentum and leaves the shaft free for your fingers to turn it. Taking care in the winding-on process to make a smooth tapering cone will help you retrieve your yarn from the spindle when it is full.

## DROP SPINDLE

Very quickly, you'll be ready to put the spinning and drafting actions together to try your spindle as a **drop spindle**. Instead of sitting and holding the spindle between your knees, try drafting while it is spinning around. Give the spindle a good clockwise twist and let it drop away from you. Use both hands near the drafting zone, the left to control the fiber supply, and the right, about 6 inches below it, to tug down gently on the newly spun yarn. Remind yourself to let the twist travel through your fingers after each quick tug or your yarn will slip apart from lack of twist. Your yarn now has to be strong enough to support the weight of the spindle, so it will constantly need the strength from the twist. Keep on spinning lengths and winding them on until you have nearly a full spindle of handspun yarn.

## BROKEN YARNS

If your yarn breaks and the spindle drops to the ground, it's because there is not enough twist in the yarn to hold it together. You may have let the yarn get too thin (thin yarn needs more twist to hold together), or you may have kept the twist from getting past your fingers into the drafted portion of fibers. Sometimes spinners will concentrate so much on the yarn they are making that they forget to check on the spindle. If it stops and then begins to unwind, your yarn will untwist and fall apart.

Don't worry, though. There will be many times when you'll want to fix a broken end or add new fiber to the end of yarn. All you have to do is make a **join**.

## MAKING JOINS

A join should be a smooth, invisible blending of fibers that is just as strong as the rest of your yarn. You make a join by overlapping a fluff of fibers from the end of the yarn to a fluff of fibers attached to the fiber supply, drafting the two fluffs together to the size of yarn you want and then letting them twist together. Place the new fibers over the old fibers by two or three inches, pinch each end of the overlap, draft to the appropriate size, and let the twist from the yarn run into the join. Add more twist by spinning the spindle, and then continue spinning the new length of yarn.

It is very important that you don't try to make a join by twisting a new fluff of fibers over an already spun portion of yarn. Doing so only lays the new fiber on top of the old yarn, and it will easily slip or rub off. Instead, join unspun fibers to unspun fibers, *draft them together*, and then add twist.

To get a nice fluffy section at the end of your yarn, untwist the fibers and spread them out. Sometimes this is easiest if you go back several inches to a place where there is a natural thickening of the yarn, a **slub**. Untwist your yarn there and fluff out the fiber ends for the join (break off and discard the few remaining inches of yarn).

*Test your join* by pulling gently on the yarn to either side to be sure the join doesn't slip apart. Then run your fingers back and forth over the join; if you see a group of fibers being pushed up into a little bundle, your join is not quite secure. Start over, joining fluff to fluff.

Joins are so important, and will be needed so often, that you should really stop and practice several now. Not only will you have occasional broken ends, but you'll also need to start a new fiber supply when you run out. Or you'll want to add different fibers or different colors when you begin to explore yarn design. Learn how to make your joins correctly in the beginning and you'll be very happy with the quality of your yarn.

Let the twist run into the join, then add more twist by spinning the spindle before you continue making the new length of yarn.

Your join will not be secure if you try to lap a fluff over a section of spun yarn. It may hold and you may be able to successfully continue spinning.

However, when you test the join by pulling the yarn or by rubbing your fingers over it, you'll discover that the yarn is not sound.

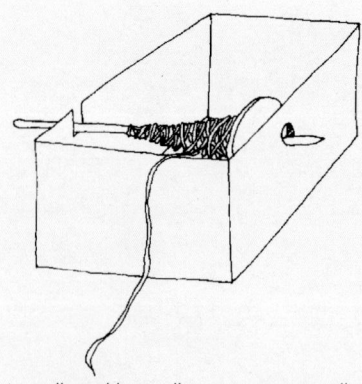

*A cardboard box will support your spindle as you wind the yarn off.*

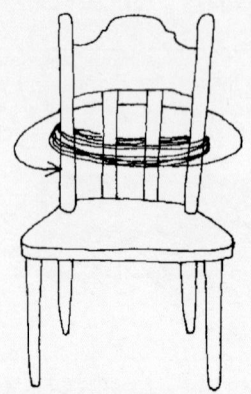

*A chair with straight sides provides a handy form for skein-winding.*

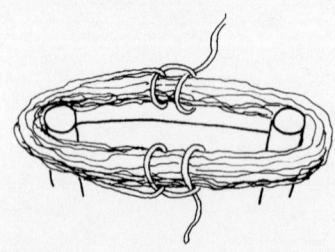

*Use the ends of your yarn to tie two half-hitch knots around the skein. You'll be able to find the ends easily this way, and your yarn will be secure as you wash it or store it for future use.*

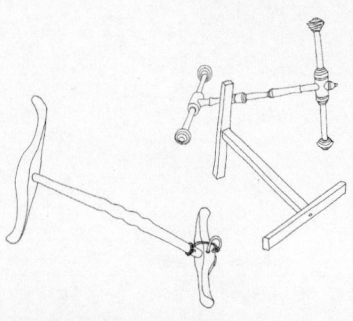

*Whether plain or fancy, every niddy-noddy has a center post, which you hold, and two end pieces (set at right angles both to the center post and to each other) around which you wind your yarn.*

## More Problems and Solutions

If the yarn seems to be getting too thin, slow down your drafting slightly. Slowing down lets the twist build up a bit so that more fibers are caught in the twist and pulled along into the forming yarn. If your yarn is getting too thick, draft a little faster and slow down the twist by turning the spindle a little slower. Make your changes gradually so that you can control them easily.

If you can't get the fibers to draft, then you may still be grasping them too tightly and too near the drafting zone. Relax your fingers and move them a couple of inches back into the fiber supply. Let the sensitivity in your fingers tell you when the fibers are loose enough to slip, but not so loose that the twist can't immediately catch them.

Don't worry about your yarn being uneven at this point. Slubs, those thicker places in your yarn, are found in every spinner's first efforts. Just work toward that feeling of smoothly flowing fibers, and that feeling in turn will smooth out the size of your yarn. If a slub is too big to ignore, stop and untwist it from both ends until the fibers are parallel, draft the fibers to the size you want, and then let the twist reenter the yarn. Fix the places that are too thin by breaking the yarn and finding a good place to make a join.

# Processing Your First Yarn

When you have a spindle full of yarn, you'll be ready to wind it off into a **skein**. You do this in order to measure the yarn's length, keep it manageable, and to **set the twist** by washing it. Winding the yarn into a skein keeps the yarn orderly and easy to handle.

First you'll want to be sure that the yarn will pull off smoothly from the spindle. If your cone of yarn is wound neatly, the yarn will pull directly off the tip of the spindle. You only have to hold the spindle still in an upright position so that your hands are free to wind and guide the yarn. You can do this by holding the spindle between your feet, knees, or two books. If you have a hook at the top of the spindle, you may find that the yarn gets caught in the hook when it tries to unwind. In that case, wind the yarn off from the side of the spindle shaft, the way you would unwind a spool of thread. Take a cardboard box and make a notch on one side and a hole in the other side to hold the spindle horizontally. It will then rotate easily as you pull the yarn, and it will leave your hands free.

### Winding the Skein

An easy way to wind your yarn into a skein is to use the back of a chair. Hold the end of the yarn securely in one place and wind the yarn from your spindle around and around the back of the chair. Don't wind it too tight, just use moderate and even tension—you want to be able to lift the whole skein from the back of the chair when you're done. When you come to the end of the yarn, tie it with the first end around the skein using two half hitch knots to keep the yarns organized and the ends easy to find.

Before you remove the skein from the back of the chair, do two more things. Measure the distance around the chair with a tape measure (in inches), and then count the number of loops in the skein (that is to say, the number of revolutions the yarn made around the chair back). Multiply the first number by the second, and you will have the length of your yarn in inches. Divide by 36, and you'll have your yardage. Keep track of the number of yards you have available, and you will soon get a feeling for how many yards you need for simple projects like hats, scarves, and mittens.

Pictured here is a *niddy-noddy*, an ancient tool used to simultaneously measure yardage and make a skein. Niddy-noddies come in various sizes, and can be crude or elegant, but most are made so that the skein length will be some portion of a yard (e.g., ½ yard, 1 yard, 1½ yards, or 2 yards). With a niddy-noddy you count the revolutions you make going around it and multiply by the niddy-noddy's size to have your yardage.

To use the niddy-noddy, hold the yarn end against the center shaft with your left hand. Use your right hand to guide the yarn around: first up and over the arm to the right, down and under the arm to the rear, up and over the arm to the left, and finally down and under the arm in front to complete the circuit. You'll have to twist and turn the niddy-noddy a little with your wrist as you go, but don't loosen your grip on the beginning of the yarn and the center shaft. Keep traveling in the same path over and over until you run out of yarn. Double check that you followed the path correctly all the way through by looking for crossed threads. Make half hitch knots around the skein with the ends as before and slip the skein off the arms of the niddy-noddy. (Sometimes the arms are removable and sometimes the arm ends are rounded down so you can slip the skein off easily.)

## SETTING THE TWIST

**Setting the twist** or **blocking** gives the fibers in the yarn a "memory" of their new position so that they stay put and do not try to untwist. Setting is done in a variety of ways depending on the fiber used. For wool yarns, the process is fast and simple. First fill a dishpan half full of very warm water (just comfortable to the hand) and some mild dishwashing detergent (don't make suds). Use only a little detergent if your fiber was clean to begin with, more if you started with greasy wool. Lay your skein on top of the water and let it sink as it absorbs water. Don't worry if your skein looks like a bunch of curly springs—the ties will help you keep it orderly. Just let the skein soak there for a few minutes to be sure the water has fully penetrated the fibers. This soaking will also clean any excess dirt or oils from the wool.

Do not be tempted to wring, scrub, or twist the skein, because too much agitation, especially in the presence of heat and moisture, will cause your yarn to felt together—and the felting process is not reversible. For the same reason, you want to avoid running water directly onto your yarn. You may, however, gently squeeze the skein once or twice.

You may notice that the yarn fluffs up or **blooms** a bit in the water—that is to be expected, and is desired by knitters and crocheters because it produces a yarn with a better **hand** (a softer, loftier feel). The fluffing is caused by the wool fibers relaxing, trying to get back to their original crimpy shape on the sheep. Fluffing is an added benefit to the finishing process.

Now lift the skein out of the wash bath and gently squeeze out the soapy water. Rinse and refill the dishpan with rinse water, the same temperature as the soapy bath. (Sudden changes in temperature can also cause felting.) Lay the skein back in the water and let it rest a few minutes more. Gently squeeze it out once or twice under the water to get rid of the soap and then lift it from the rinse bath. Gently squeeze out the water and roll the skein in a fresh, clean cotton towel to absorb the excess moisture.

Once it's rinsed, gently straighten the skein to its original coiled form between your two hands. If the yarn will be used for knitting or crocheting, simply lay the skein on a fresh, dry towel (away from sun, wind, and pets) and let it dry, turning it occasionally. Drying will take about a day, depending on the climate and weather.

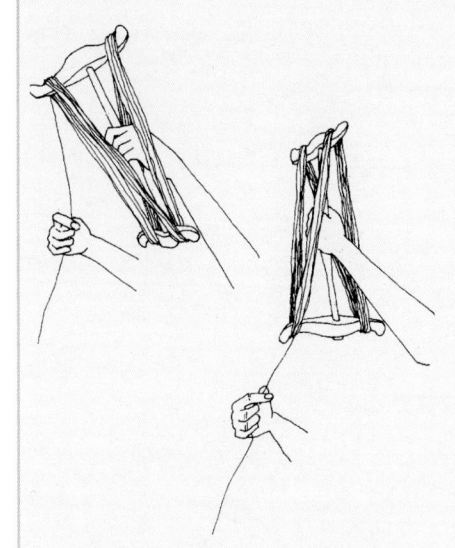

After a little trial and error, you'll be able to smoothly rotate the niddy-noddy and wind your yarn into a skein.

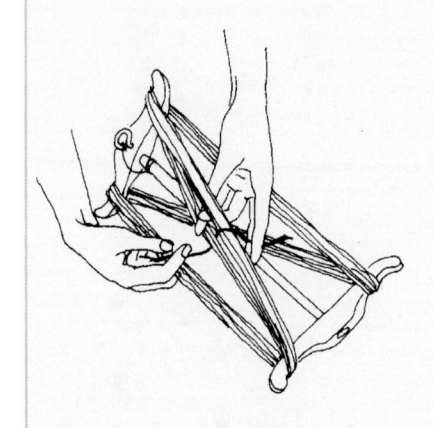

Check that no threads have been crossed and then use the ends of yarn to make two half hitch knots.

Dry your yarn under tension to set the twist by hanging it with a towel through the skein to provide weight. Shift the skein and towel as the skein dries to help it dry faster.

Making a skein

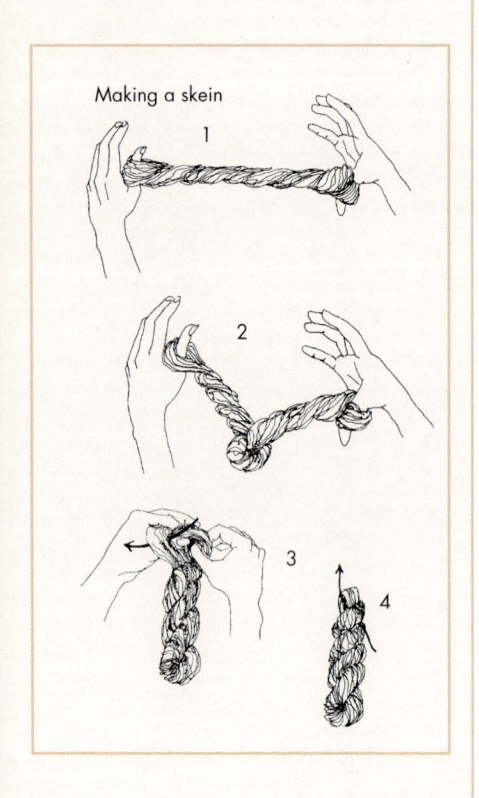

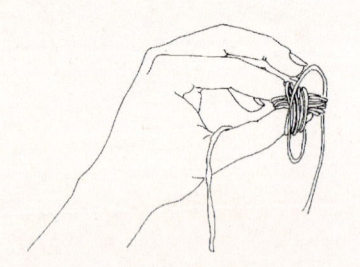

Begin winding a center-pull ball with a figure eight around two fingers. Then fold and pinch this center section before you continue to wind.

Ply from two balls back onto your spindle, but turn the spindle in the opposite direction that you spun your singles. Keep the balls in bowls to keep them from rolling all over the place.

### DRYING UNDER TENSION

If you plan to use your yarn for weft in weaving, you may want it to dry under tension. Drying the yarn under tension eliminates all or most of the kinks in the yarn, but too much tension discourages loft.

To apply tension, slip the top of the skein over a hook or pole. Place a folded towel through the bottom of the skein. The weight should be just enough to keep the skein straight. Shift the skein and towel occasionally so that the skein dries evenly.

### MAKING A SKEIN

A clean, dry skein can be stored in its own neat package. (1) Hold the skein in front of you under a little tension with your hands apart and your thumbs holding the skein. (2) Rotate your right thumb counterclockwise so that the skein begins to twist on itself. (3) When the twisted loops are fairly tight around your thumbs, let the skein fold in half and (4) put one end through the other. The skein will find its own equilibrium in this twisted state and the secured loop will keep it from coming undone. Be sure not to twist it too much or you will compress the loft.

### MAKING A BALL

When you are ready to work with your yarn, you'll want to wind it into a ball. You can simply place the skein over the back of a chair, remove the ties, and begin winding a ball by hand. To wind a ball that pulls from the center (keeping the yarn neat and tidy and the ball stationary), try this method. First start winding a figure eight between your thumb and little finger. After ten wraps, take the figure eight and fold it in half upon itself, saving out an eight-inch length of yarn from the starting end. Holding the starting end out of the way, pinch the folded figure eight together with thumb and forefinger and begin wrapping yarn around both fingers and yarn folds. After about ten wraps, remove your fingers, change positions, and begin wrapping in the same direction. Change positions frequently and always wrap around two or three fingers *and* the ball of yarn. Wrapping around your fingers keeps your yarn from a wrap so tight that it compresses the loft. Make sure that the starting end is still available—that's the end you'll start from when you use the ball.

## Plying on Your Spindle

The skein of yarn you just made with one strand is called a **singles** yarn. Plying is the process of respinning two or more singles yarns together into a larger yarn. One of the most common plied yarns for spinners is a two-ply yarn: Two singles yarns, both spun with a Z twist, are spun together in the opposite direction with an S twist. Plying both strengthens the yarn and evens out size and twist irregularities.

By plying in the opposite direction from the original twist, you make two things happen. First, the Z-twist and the S-twist energies tend to neutralize one another. If it's done just right, the result is a **balanced** yarn—one without excess twist energy one direction of the other. Second, since the single yarns are partially untwisting as they are plied, the two-ply yarn looks and feels softer than the original singles. If you are going to make a plied yarn, you need to spin the yarn with more twist than if you were going to leave it as a singles. Wash your yarn *after* it is plied and not before.

Here are two methods to try on your handspindle.

In the first plying method, you start with two balls of singles. Put each in a bowl or basket to control its movement as it unwinds. Next attach the ends of both yarns to your spindle as if they were one yarn. Spiral the yarn up the shaft (remember to turn your spindle *counterclockwise* this time, in the S-twist direction) and secure it under the hook or make a half hitch as necessary. Ply the two yarns together in the S-twist direction (counterclockwise). Wind on as before, in the same direction used for plying.

The second method of plying, *Andean plying*, is especially useful if you have only one spindle. (1)Loop the end of the yarn over your thumb and wind off the singles yarn from your spindle onto your hand by (2)going around the back of your hand and around, and looping over your middle finger, (3)around the back of your hand, (4)over your middle finger again, and (5)back around the back of your hand. Keep track of the ends. When you've wound off all the yarn onto your hand, and (6)have removed it from your middle finger to your wrist, (7)take both ends and (8)spin them together in the opposite direction from the singles.

## More on Balanced Yarns

Balanced yarns work very well in many woven, knitted, and crocheted projects. A plied yarn doesn't need to be exactly balanced to perform well, since washing and drying will set the twist and make the yarn quite tame. Just aim for a naturally balanced yarn, checking it as you go, and it will work very well. To check to see if your yarn is balanced, unwind a two-foot length of the plied yarn and hold it between your hands. Move your hands together to create a loop and watch to see if the yarns want to twist around each other or not. Add or subtract twist to balance the yarn and then test it again.

Balanced, handspun yarns can be softer, much more elastic, and have more body than similar commercial yarns. If your yarn isn't balanced, whether it's a singles or plied, it can cause your finished project to slant in one direction; no amount of blocking can fix it.

# Fiber Preparations

There are a number of ways in which fibers can be prepared for spinning, some of them quite simple, some very involved. The aim of preparation is to make the fibers suitable for drafting with the degree of control you want. The more careful and thorough the preparation, the more control you have over the size and texture of the yarn. Basically the better the fiber preparation, the easier it is to spin.

Fiber preparations fall into two major categories: *carded* and *combed*. These terms are used to describe not only the preparation of wool, but that of cotton, silk, and other fiber as well. The two types of preparation affect the kind of yarn that can be spun, so it is important to become familiar with them.

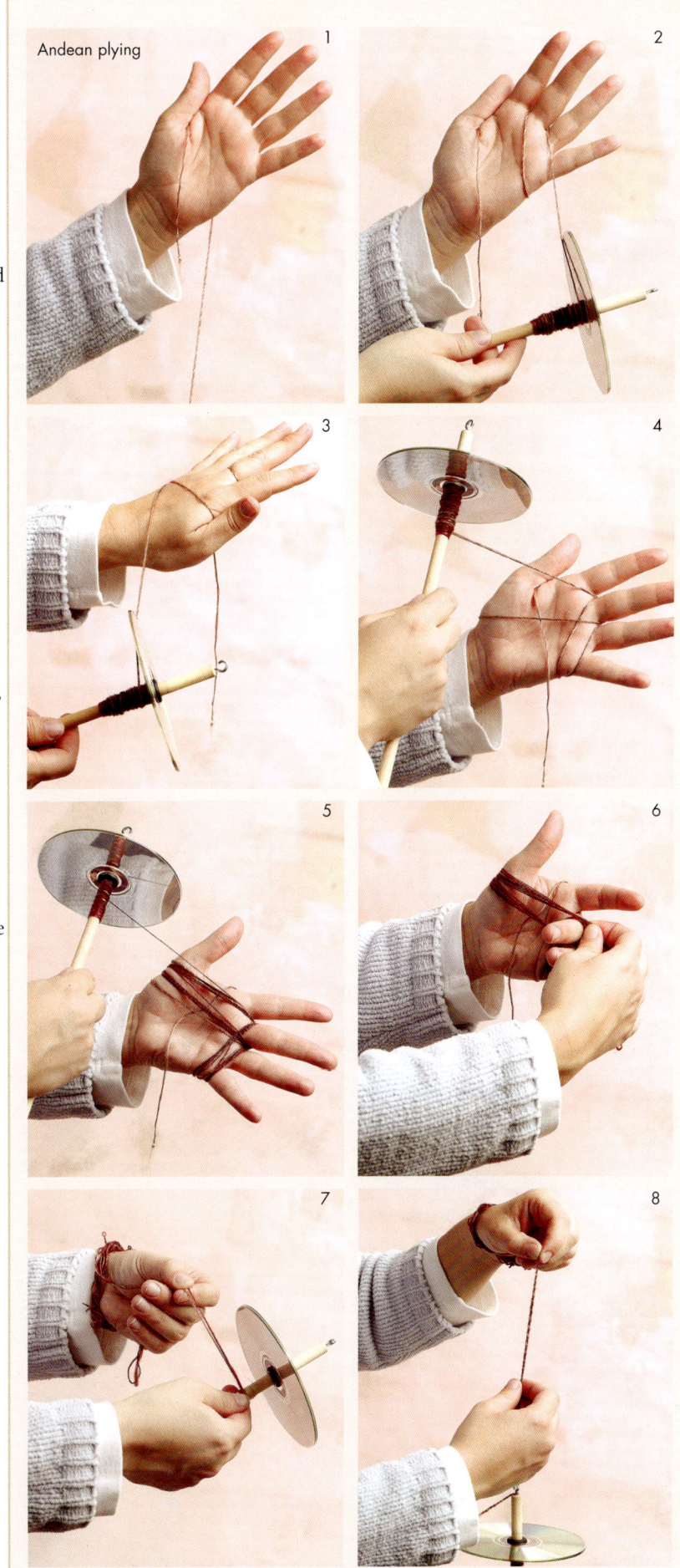

Andean plying

This is all wool! It has been prepared for spinning in a number of different ways. There are (1) rolags, (2) a carded batt, (3) roving, (4) pencil roving, (5) flicked locks, and (6) tops.

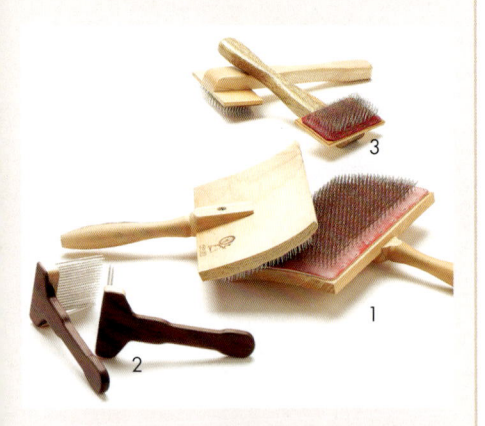

Prepare fiber for spinning by using tools such as (1) handcards, (2) mini combs, (3) 2 flick carders, (4) drumcarder, and (5) cotton handcards.

**Carded** fibers result in **woolen** yarns: soft, lofty, fuzzy yarns (made of any fiber) that contain many fiber lengths. The fibers are first washed and dried, then brushed over opposing sets of short wire teeth to open and separate the fibers into a uniform mass.

Carded preparations from mills are called **slivers**, **batts**, or **rovings**, depending how they look when they come off the carding machine. Slivers (pronounced *sly*vers) are thick, long, continuous strands of carded wool. They contain no twist. Slivers need no further preparation and can be spun directly from the end. Batts are thick cushiony rectangles made of thin layers of carded wool. They can be torn into strips or separated into layers for spinning, or they can be used for felting or padding. Rovings (*row*vings) are very similar to slivers, but they are much thinner and contain a slight amount of twist. A pencil roving is about as thick as a pencil, and is usually spun without further drafting.

Carded preparations that you make at home are called batts or **rolags** (*roll*ags). Batts are made on small tabletop carding machines usually cranked by hand. Batts are small and, depending on the machine, may need to be put through several times for the wool to be uniformly blended. Rolags are made with a set of **handcarders**, two paddle boards faced with closely set rows of fine wire teeth. The fibers are brushed and opened with the carders and then rolled into big cigar shapes of fluffy wool.

**Combed** fibers result in **worsted** yarns: strong, smooth, shiny yarns that contain only long fibers. In mills, combed fibers first go through the carding process to open them up, and then they are combed so that the short or broken fibers are removed and the remaining long fibers are left lying parallel to one another. Combing is done at home with a pair of **wool combs**. Each comb has rows of long sharpened tines which separate and align the fibers, removing short fibers and tangles in the process. Whether formed at the mill or at home, combed preparations are called **tops**.

### THE CARDING PROCESS

You'll be able to find handcarders in spinning and weaving shops, or by mail order from *Spin·Off* or other fiber magazines. You'll often be given a choice between straight-backed carders or curved-back carders, and between wool carders or cotton carders. For your first pair, I suggest that you get curved-back wool carders. The curved backs will give you precise control during the carding process, and the wool carders (also called wool cards) handle a wide range of fiber types and diameters. Later on, when you want to experiment with carding and blending short delicate fibers like cotton, some of the silks, cashmere, and Angora rabbit, you'll want to invest in cotton carders with finer closer-set teeth.

The purpose of hand carding is to open, separate, and straighten the wool fibers. The product is a small batt or rolag of wool whose openness and loftiness makes your drafting much easier. Hand carding also gives you greater control in spinning the woolen yarn you desire. Woolen yarns are warm because air is trapped among the fibers; they are fuzzier at the surface than worsted yarns, and they're generally softer and loftier. Woolen yarns are excellent for knitting and crocheting and as the weft yarns in weaving.

The first thing to do is **charge** a handcarder with wool (1). Take one carder in your left hand, palm up, with the handle pointing away from you and the wooden back resting against your leg (wire teeth pointing up). This left carder will remain stationary while the other carder does the work. Take a little clean wool in your right hand and begin pulling it across the teeth of the left carder from the handle end toward the front end, so that the fibers are just held by the teeth. Load it until the teeth are barely obscured—

you can card a thin layer more efficiently and evenly than a thick layer. Fiber ends should extend beyond the front edge of the carder, but they should not extend beyond the teeth at the handle end (2).

Now take the other carder in your right hand, palm down, with the handle toward you and the wood back facing up (3). You are going to brush the wool on the left carder with the right carder, using a gentle rocking motion, so that the teeth at the handle end of the right carder engage the wool first. As you rock through and brush back, the front teeth engage the wool last.

When you get to the point in your stroke where the teeth meet, avoid pulling *down* and through so that the teeth interlock and end up scraping past one another. Instead, just pull *back* and through so that the teeth barely touch as they pass.

On your successive strokes continue the rocking motion as you brush the wool. Brush the wool that lies on *top* of the teeth, not the wool imbedded *in* the teeth. If you mesh the teeth of the carders together and forcefully pull them past one another, you will end up tearing and breaking the delicate fibers. You will also put excessive wear on your carders.

It will take about five to ten strokes to transfer the wool from the left carder onto the right carder. When all the wool on top of the teeth has been carded, and both carders look equally charged, it is time to start *lifting* and brushing the remaining fibers from the teeth of the left carder as they transfer to the right carder (4).

Transfer the wool from the left carder to the right carder by starting at the front edge and engaging the fiber tips hanging off the front end of the left carder as before, but do not stroke back. Instead, rock the right carder forward, meshing some of the teeth of the two carders together (but not scraping them past one another). *Lift* the right carder from the handle toward its front edge as you pull through and complete your rocking stroke—the engaged fibers from the left carder will lift from the teeth and surface of that card and transfer to the right carder.

You need to go through the whole process once or twice more, or as many times as necessary to open and brush the fibers into a completely uniform mass. To start again, *transfer* the fibers on the right carder back onto the left carder as follows. Turn the right carder face up. Holding the carders perpendicular to one another, begin to lift the fiber ends extending from the front end of the right carder with the back teeth of the left carder. When the front end of the

**1**
Charge the carder by taking a handful of wool and pulling it across the teeth of the carder. Do this gently; brush the wool across the teeth and let them grab a part of it.

**2**
Repeat until you have a thin, even layer of wool across the carder.

**3**
Begin to card by taking the other carder in your right hand. Use a light, rocking motion. The tips of the teeth on the carders should not meet.

**4**
When your wool appears to be evenly divided between the carders, lift and transfer the remaining fibers on the left carder to the right carder.

**5**
Repeat steps 3 and 4 until the fibers are blended, then transfer the carded batt from the left to the right carder.

**6**
Lay the carded batt on the surface of the left carder.

15

7

Use the edge of the right carder and your left hand to start rolling the rolag.

When you are ready to spin, join the fibers from one end of a rolag to your yarn and begin.

It's very satisfying to have a basket of rolags ready to spin. Once you have the idea of carding, you will find room for a lot of creativity in this process. The rolags below are the result of a color blending experiment.

right carder meets the middle of the left carder, push the teeth of the carders together briefly so that the teeth of the left carder can get a better grip. Then you can continue to gently lift the fibers from the teeth of the right carder. All the fibers should now be resting lightly on top of the left carder (you may have a line of fibers down the middle that are more imbedded in the teeth). Now you just have to secure the fibers in the teeth of the left carder, which you can do by pressing them down with your hand, or with the back of the right carder.

Repeat the carding process as described until the fibers are straight and uniformly opened. Generally, two or three times through is sufficient.

To remove the wool from the right carder when you are finished, just lift it as you did before with the teeth of the left carder (5). You can then use the teeth of the right carder to lift any remaining wool from the left carder to be sure all the fibers are free. This time, though, there is no need to dig the teeth in for a better hold. You should now have a little batt of wool resting freely on top of the teeth of the right carder.

Starting with the fiber tips farthest from you, start rolling the wool jellyroll fashion toward you (6). As you roll with your fingers, keep the ends of the roll from expanding by controlling them with the heels of your hands. When you have the cigar shape completely rolled, pick it up, place it at the end of the carder farthest from you again, and once more roll it down toward you with just a bit of pressure (7). This second roll will help compact the rolag and seal the free edge of the roll so it holds its rounded shape.

You can make a basketful of rolags at your leisure, and then sit down to spin. Pick one up, join the fibers from one end to your leader, and begin spinning. When you near the end of one rolag, pick up another, make a good join with the first, and continue.

Once you understand the basic carding process you will begin to see all sorts of possibilities for blending colors on the carders. You can thinly layer the colors on top of one another or place them side by side. Card thoroughly for a uniform blend and a heathered effect in your yarn. Card less completely for a stippled effect. Or make a basketful of colored rolags that you pick up randomly and spin for a variegated effect.

## PROBLEMS IN CARDING

1) If you are too vigorous in your carding, especially when you're using the finer wools, you will find that you are making a lot of little tangled knots in the wool that are impossible to get out. These are called **neps** or **noils**, and they are bits of broken and damaged fiber that tangle and cling together. Avoid making neps by carding gently, being especially careful to avoid intermeshing the card teeth and raking them past one another. Card as you would brush a small child's hair.

Another way that neps are formed is by starting a new carding stroke before the first one is completely finished. Be sure that there are no fibers still connecting the two carders at the end of a stroke before you return for another. Otherwise you'll be folding the fibers over on top of themselves and inviting tangles to form.

Neps are a common problem in home carding, cottage industry carding, and industrial carding, so don't worry if you see some in your own wool. In fact, some spinners rather like the texture that neps add to the batt or rolag and the subsequent yarn. Just be aware that you will definitely end up with a textured yarn and not a smooth one. And neps, because they rest on the outside of the yarn, can make your sweater or hat look like it has already started pilling (pilling is the formation of small tenacious tangles of fibers on the surface of fabrics—a phenomenon caused by friction and wear).

2) If you let the fiber ends extend beyond the teeth at the handle end of the carder, they will tend to wrap around those teeth as carding progresses. This leaves a visible line of looped fibers that make it hard to get a uniformly open batt of wool. Take care to keep the fibers straight and always well in front of the teeth near the handle.

3) If you put too much wool on your carder, it will take you much longer to do the job. You will also be much less thorough, and you are likely to end up with neps as you work hard to control the unruly strands.

4) The teeth on your carders may feel quite stiff when they are new. Ideally, you want some "give" in the teeth so they move back and forth a bit in their **carding cloth** (the backing that the teeth are attached to). Teeth that are inflexible do damage to the wool fibers. With use, the teeth on your cards will become more flexible, but it's a good idea to test their flexibility before you buy. They should move about a quarter inch when you flex them back and forth with your thumb. For wool cards, look for teeth about the size of a straight pin or finer, set about an eighth-inch apart.

## Combing

More spinners today prepare their wool by carding than by combing, even though combing goes back farther in history.

Wool combs vary in price and type, and are usually considered more suitable for the intermediate spinner than for the beginner. However, a basic understanding of the principles of combing will give you an overall understanding of spinning methods.

Combing, like carding, opens and straightens fibers for the spinning process. But combing has the additional advantage of separating out the short and weak fibers from the long and strong fibers. At the end of the combing process, you have two products instead of one: **noils**, the short and tangled fibers, and a combed **top**, the parallel arrangement of the long and strong fibers. The noils can be saved to card with other noils or with other woolen preparations for woolen yarns; the top is used to spin worsted yarn. Worsted yarn is stronger, smoother, more lustrous, and more distinct in the fabric structure than the same yarn prepared and spun woolen. Hand woolcombing opens up a whole new side of wool preparation to handspinners.

Wool combs look more menacing than carders, as you can see. They can have anywhere from one to eight rows of teeth (referred to as the "pitch") though three to five rows are usual. Carefully cleaned wool is **loaded** (or **lashed**) onto the first row or two of teeth of the stationary comb (clamped onto a table). The moveable comb is then used to comb gradually from the tips to the base of the fibers, much as you would comb long tangled hair. As the work progresses, the wool gradually transfers to the moving comb, and then back again to the stationary comb. Once the wool is completely opened and all the noils are caught back in the tines of the combs, the long fibers are **drawn off** into a top through the eye of a **diz**, and the noils are left behind. A diz is an oval disk with a concave curve and a hole in the center used create a consistent top of combed fibers. With practice, hand combing can produce prepared fibers more efficiently than hand carding.

## Semi-worsted Preparations

Although combs are unique in their effectiveness, there are other small tools—such as a dog comb or a **wool hackle**—that you can use to separate short fibers from long ones while you are opening and straightening fibers. A wool hackle has longer teeth than a dog comb, usually in one or two rows. With this tool, you can open the fibers and leave them lashed on, then draw them off into a top with a diz.

Wool combs and mini combs produce a very even preparation. After combing has been completed, the wool is drawn off the combs into a top.

*Use a flicker to open individual locks by striking the tip end of the lock with the flicker. Wear jeans or protect your leg with a piece of leather.*

*Recondition commercially processed sliver or roving by holding it with your hands about six inches apart and gently snapping the fiber.*

*If you pull too hard or place your hands too far apart when you condition the sliver, it will become thin in places.*

### FLICKING

The fiber-preparation technique called **flicking** employs a small tool much like a miniature wool carder. If you don't have a flicker, you can use a small dog brush or one end of your wool carders. Spinners use flicking to prepare both greasy wool and clean wool.

*Tapping method.* Have some canvas or a piece of leather that you can use to protect your leg. Take a lock of wool and lay it across your knee. Holding it very firmly at the shorn end, tap the flicker through the tips of the lock and pull up and back in a quick motion. The movements are primarily up and down rather than back and forth. Work your way up to the shorn end, reverse the lock, and flick the shorn end as well. This method lifts and separates the fibers as they are being brushed and seems to be a bit easier on the fiber than the brushing method.

*Brushing method.* Instead of tapping up and down with the flicker, begin at the tip ends and just brush through the fibers. Work your way up the lock, reverse it, and flick/brush the shorn end. This method may be a bit more effective in removing dry, weathered tips from the wool, but you may well end up with more broken fibers in the teeth of the flicker than you would with the tapping method.

### CONDITIONING A COMMERCIAL SLIVER OR ROVING

Mill-produced slivers and rovings can become very compact by the time they reach you, through packaging, shipping, repackaging, and just plain old age. There is a quick way to "recondition" them that will make drafting much easier and more pleasurable. This method works for commercially combed tops as well.

Grasp the sliver or roving at one end, with your hands about six inches apart. Gently snap the sliver four or five times until you feel the fibers just start to "give" or slip past one another. You don't want to thin or pull apart the sliver at all, you just want to get the fibers to barely start slipping past one another. Move both hands down one or two inches (no more) and repeat. As you go, you'll notice the sliver starting to loft and soften. You need to do only as much as you plan to spin for that session, since the rest can still be stored compactly and reconditioned as needed.

Slivers and tops are usually spun from the end, but some spinners prefer to split the top lengthwise. This approach gives better control during drafting since you are not working with as much fiber at a time. First break off a three-foot length of top like this: Grasp the top on either side of the three-foot mark, with your hands six to eight inches apart. Gently pull the fibers until they completely come apart. If the fibers won't budge, you are holding your hands too close together. Take the piece of top and hold it up to the light to find a naturally thin section running lengthwise. Separate the top there with a snapping motion, rather than pulling both sides gradually apart. In this way, you will minimize the disruption of fibers along the lengthwise break. Split the section of top as many as three times and spin each section from the end.

## Yarn Finishing

An important factor that contributes to a yarn's behavior and appearance is **finishing**, the processes you put the yarn through before you use it. Finishing steps can include washing, rinsing, dyeing, steaming, weighting, blocking, and setting the twist. The whole idea is to get the yarn to its finished state *before* it goes into your project—you don't want any surprises when your project is first wetted or washed.

The most important finishing step is setting the twist. Setting the twist in a yarn can be done in a variety of ways, depending on the fiber and how permanent the set needs to be. The most common method is washing.

Merely leaving yarn on the bobbin for a few days gives it a temporary set that often makes it easier to handle for plying or skeining. A more permanent set results from washing or steaming.

Steaming the wool fibers for two minutes or longer will actually break old chemical bonds and form new ones, changing the internal structure of fibers to conform to their new shape. To steam your yarn, you can hold a taut skein over a steaming tea kettle for several minutes. Use a niddy-noddy or two sticks to hold the skein while you steam it. Be very careful to keep your hands and arms out of the way—steam burns happen in an instant and are quite painful. The skein can be left on the niddy-noddy or laid on a towel to dry.

Another, and safer, steaming method employs a hand-held steamer from a fabric or small-appliance store. Wind the yarn on a reel or niddy-noddy and gradually go around the skein with the steamer so that every part is thoroughly steamed. Then leave the yarn on the reel or niddy-noddy to dry.

After washed or steamed silk yarn has dried, it may feel stiff. The softness will come back as it is handled.

## STORING YOUR WOOL AND YARN

It would be lovely if we could display all our handspun wool yarns in baskets around the house, since they're beautiful to look at and inspire us with project ideas. The danger, however, is that your precious handspun skeins, and your unspun wool, whether washed or unwashed, will become a feast for the two kinds of pests that are the spinner's bane.

The most common pest is the wool moth, whose larvae dine on our fine woolens. There are two types of wool moths to watch out for: the casemaking clothes moth and the webbing clothes moth. In both cases the adults are tiny (one-quarter-inch long) buff-colored moths that seem to dart rapidly and randomly around a room, especially in the warmer months, as they seek a nice warm, dark place to lay their eggs. These larvae eat any animal fiber except silk.

The other pest, which we don't hear about as often but which is just as destructive, is the carpet beetle. Like wool moth larvae, carpet beetle larvae feed on protein. They are often found under carpets and in the cracks and crevices of flooring. Carpet beetle larvae eat all the protein fibers—including silk. The adults are roundish, hard-shelled beetles about one-eighth inch in diameter, and they are a mottled brown color. The larvae are about one-fourth inch long and have black bristles. The best safeguards against moth and carpet beetle damage (besides the poisons like mothballs) are careful storage and constant vigilance. The larvae don't like light or moving air; if you go through your stored fibers and garments regularly, you can air them out and inspect for early warning signs.

If you *do* find signs of infestation, take the fibers outside immediately. If damage is extensive, throw the fiber in the outside garbage. If damage is minor, you can try drowning the eggs and larvae by submerging the fibers for twelve hours or more, or you can freeze them at near 0°F for several days.

Store wool and other protein fibers in paper bags that are taped shut (larvae don't eat the cellulose of paper bags), and then put them in cardboard cartons. Label the bags and cartons with the contents, and put a small sample on the outside in a self-sealing plastic bag.

Plastic bags themselves often afford good short-term protection if wool moths or carpet beetles are not a big problem in your area (they seem to prefer low altitudes and humid climates). But moth larvae can eat through plastic bags when they're hungry enough.

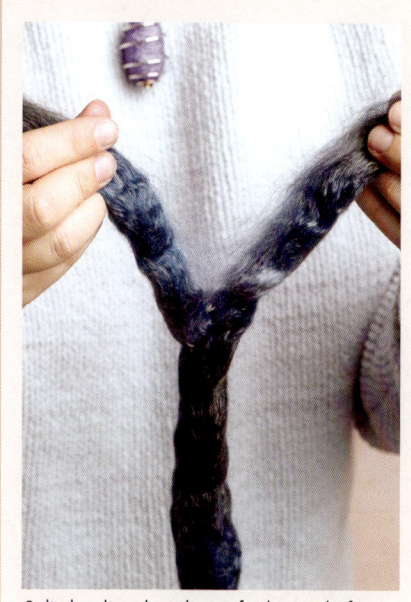

Split the sliver lengthwise for better drafting control.

Use a nøstepinne to make a center pull ball of yarn.

Fragrant herbs such as lavender, rosemary, and cloves can also be successful in discouraging moth and carpet beetle infestation. Be sure to freshen the sachets often, and place them and your fibers in a tightly closed box or chest to contain the vapors.

Cellulose (plant) fibers are rarely attacked by insects. Silverfish, crickets, cockroaches, and termites may chew a few holes in these fabrics (especially if they are starched), but they find most of their food elsewhere. You do have to be concerned with mildew and funguses, though, so keep cellulose fibers dry and expose them to sunlight from time to time.

# Wool

**Wool** is the downy or hairy outer coat grown by sheep. Some older breeds of sheep grow both: a downy undercoat and a long hairy outer coat. Most modern breeds now have a single coat. The length of the sheared fiber, called the **staple length**, can be from two to fifteen inches, depending on the breed; the diameter, luster, crimp, and color can vary just as much. Washed wool varies in color from a creamy white through tans and browns, and from silver through grays and black.

*Crimp*, the three-dimensional waviness along the length of the fiber, is a naturally occurring property of wool. Crimp adds a little extra friction between fibers and creates a lofty yarn. Finely crimped wool is associated with short stapled fleeces of fine diameter; the crimp on long luster wools looks more like long open curls.

Fine, short wools, like Merino, Romney, Rambouillet, and Cormo, are suitable for very soft garments worn next to the skin. Prepare these wools carefully to avoid neps, and spin them to a fine diameter.

Cross-bred and medium-length wools, like Corriedale, Columbia, Polwarth, Finn, and Perendale, make excellent handspinning fleeces. These wools are used extensively for sweaters, hats, mittens, gloves, and jackets—almost all outer wear. Some of the finer and first clip fleeces (the first fleece sheared from a year-old animal is called a *hoggett* fleece) can often be used for next-to-the-skin wear as well. These are good fleeces for the beginner.

Shortwool and down breeds, like Suffolk, Hampshire, Dorset, and Jacob, have been used by handspinners for centuries. They are sometimes described as "spongy" in texture, and they lack the softness and sheen of the other short wools, but they are suitable for outerwear garments.

Longwool and luster breeds, including Romney, Border Leicester, Lincoln, Coopworth, and Cotswold, are much prized for their use in worsted yarns. Their length and glossy surfaces contribute to strong, lustrous yarns that can be knitted or woven for outer garments. These fibers can also be prepared and spun woolen, and some of their sheen will still show through. The fibers of the longwool breeds resemble mohair.

Coarsewool and mountain breeds include Scottish Blackface, Cheviot, Black Welsh Mountain, Karakul and Rough Fell. Their fleeces are used for hardwearing fabrics and carpets.

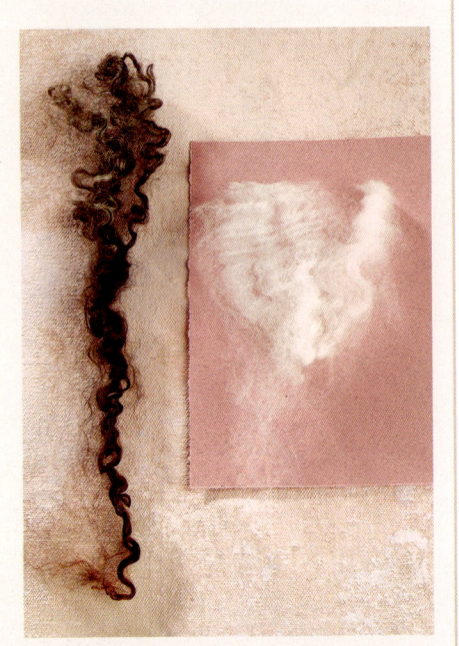

Crimp can be fine as in the right lock (New Zealand Romney), or coarse as in the left lock (Wensleydale).

An American Romney sheep from Karen Ososki and Karl Ottenstein's Spring Creek Organic Farm, Sandpoint, Idaho.

# Scouring (Washing) Your Wool

Scouring removes wool grease, suint, dirt, vegetation, chemicals, and pests from your wool before you spin it. **Wool grease** is chemically a wax, and has a melting point between 95° and 104°F. That's important to remember when you are drawing the scouring bath.

The three things you want to do in scouring your wool are (1) to get it completely clean, while you (2) avoid felting, and (3) avoid any alkaline damage.

### 1. *Getting it Clean*

The finer the fleece, the more grease it contains, and therefore the harder it is to get clean. When you have a hard-to-clean fleece, you may be tempted to agitate and scrub more, which leads to felting, or to add harsh cleaning agents, which leads to alkaline damage. And the finer the fleece, the more susceptible it is to felting and to alkaline damage.

The solution is twofold: Use *hot* water, so that the bath will not cool down too much as the wool sits and soaks, and use more detergent than you would for just about any other cleaning job. If you use the hot water right out of your tap, you'll find that it's probably somewhere between 120° and 140°F, hot enough to keep the temperature of the bath above the melting point of the grease while you work, but low enough to avoid damaging the fibers. As for the use of more detergent, it takes *fifteen to sixteen times* the amount of detergent to remove wool grease than it does for other oils and greases. If you don't use *a lot* of mild detergent when you scour, you won't get all the grease out; the wool may feel clean initially, but a few weeks later the remaining grease will oxidize and become tacky. Trying to smoothly spin a fine, tacky wool is an exercise in frustration.

Wool wax, or lanolin, does not become rancid, unlike other organic fats, but it does dry to a sticky consistency. Think about this when you are tempted to "leave some natural lanolin" in your washed fleeces for water repellency. The wool fiber's outer cuticle is already a naturally water-repellent surface. Leaving oils or grease on your wools is an invitation to rapid soiling.

And remember: Even in the wool industry's harsh scouring methods, about five percent of the grease is left in the wool. Hand scouring leaves even more. So feel free to be thorough in your washing, without any fear of drying out the fleece excessively.

### 2. *Avoiding Felting*

Felting requires moisture, heat, and agitation of the wool. A good scour also requires moisture, heat, and agitation, in the presence of a detergent. But if you concentrate on getting the temperature of the water right, using enough detergent, and limiting agitation, you can get very clean, soft wool without felting.

Some other things that you can do to avoid felting are to never run water directly on the wool, and keep the temperature of the wash and rinse baths the same.

### 3. *Alkaline Damage*

Wool can be damaged in scouring liquors that exceed 9 or 9.5 on the acid/alkaline (pH) scale. Since most of us don't use pH testers, you can see that adding washing soda to the bath can be a dangerous proposition. Although it can boost cleaning power, washing soda is highly alkaline, and alkaline solutions above pH 9.5 "eat" wool.

Alkaline damage is irreversible. It is characterized by curling tips (especially at the shorn end), scale damage (even a dissolving of the scales), and a harsh hand.

Scoured and dyed Merino wool courtesy of Cyril Lieschke, New South Wales, Australia.

## SOAPS AND DETERGENTS

Some scouring recipes recommend the use of pure soap to clean wool because of its mildness. But there are two problems with pure soaps. One is that you have to be darn sure that the soap flakes are *completely* dissolved before you put the wool into the bath. If there are semidissolved flakes in the water, they stick to the wool, and for some reason more scouring does not remove them. Even worse, pure soaps will combine with calcium and magnesium in hard water to leave insoluble precipitates—goopy little globs that tend to redeposit on the wool. They do not wash out. Once you've got them, you're stuck with them.

But all is not lost if you're in a hard-water area. All you have to do is use a mild liquid dishwashing detergent or its equivalent. These preparations contain something called "sequestrants" that bind up the minerals before the precipitates can form. Or you can use a water softener like Calgon, or any of the mechanical ion exchange systems.

Orvus® paste (sodium laurel sulfate) is a pure, mild, pH-neutral detergent. I like this very mild pure detergent for scouring. It is made of the same basic ingredient found in many shampoos. You can buy it in gallon jugs at feed stores (ranchers use Orvus to clean their animals before a show). I don't recommend Woolite® because its properties of suspension, lubrication, and protection of the fiber are less effective than some other detergents. Neither can I recommend laundry detergents—they have too many additives, some of them harsh.

## SCOURING RECIPES

1. Carefully separate a piece of fleece of the same dimensions as your dishpan: Hold the tips of the locks firmly on either side of the place where you want the fleece to separate and pull them apart. Work neatly—don't let the fibers slide past one another and become messed up. Work your way around the section of fleece until it is free from the rest. Keep all the tips facing in one direction, and the shorn ends in the other.

2. Fill two dishpans with hot water right out of the tap. Add liquid dishwashing detergent (or Orvus) to both pans until the water feels slick when tested with a clean dry hand. Do not make suds.

3. Turn the section of fleece on its side so that the tips face the center of the dishpan and the shorn edges face the side. Immerse the fleece slowly along the left edge of the first dishpan. Let it soak there for ten minutes.

4. With your left hand, push a section of wool down to the bottom of the pan. With your right hand, rub the tips of the locks of that same section of wool until they come clean. (You can agitate the tips of the locks as much as you want to, as long as the shorn ends don't move. Felting takes place at the shorn end.) Repeat until all the tips are clean.

5. Use your right hand as a barrier so the wool doesn't try to slide around and move to the right. With your left hand, slowly gather up the wool toward you until you can lift it gently from underneath. Let it drain there a bit as you hold it. Remember, wool is weak when wet, so it must be well supported. You can squeeze the wool slowly and gently to help drain off the dirty, soapy water.

6. Put the wool in the second bath in the same position (that bath should be the same temperature as the first bath). Let the wool soak for another five or ten minutes, with no agitation at all.

7. Remove the wool as you did in step five, and set it aside. Drain and rinse the dishpans. Fill them with water the same temperature as the baths you just emptied, or slightly hotter. Add about three or four tablespoons of vinegar to the first bath

Resist the temptation to agitate the wool as you wash it. Simply place the locks on the surface of the water and watch as they absorb the water and sink.

(the amount is not critical; the vinegar will help cut the excess detergent and leave the wool in a slightly acid environment).

8. Put the wool in the first rinse bath in the same position, and gently push it down slowly until it is covered. Don't let the wool migrate all over the pan. Leave it there for five minutes, and then repeat in the second rinse bath.

9. Lift the wool carefully as in step five, gently squeeze out the excess water, and lay the wool on a clean dry towel to drain. Once the towel has soaked up a good deal of the water, you can speed drying by moving the wool to a fresh dry towel. Let it dry away from heat, sun, pets, and any further agitation. Depending on the weather, it will dry completely in one to three days.

Scouring the wool this way will leave you with tips and shorn ends aligned, so that you can use the clean wool for carding or combing.

This washing sequence took you all the way through with one small section of the fleece, but you can use the sequence as a sort of wash train. If the fleece is not excessively dirty, you can use the first wash bath twice, and the successive baths as well, so that one wool section immediately follows another. If the fleece is pretty greasy and dirty, you can just replace the first wash bath with the second, and make up a new second bath. Depending on how your facilities are set up, you can use this procedure to make washing a fleece easy, fast, and water-saving.

If you have a very special fleece, either one that is very fine and delicate, or perhaps quite dirty at the tips, you may want to scour lock by lock. Separate and handle the locks individually and wash as described for washing a section of fleece. Keep the shorn ends tucked tightly away in your hand while you scrub the tips. Let the just-scrubbed locks soak undisturbed in the second bath while you scrub the next lock in the first bath.

## The End and the Beginning

This book just opens the door into the world of natural fibers and the yarns that can be made from them. There are many paths you can follow now to expand your knowledge and give you inspiration.

We have touched on getting started on a handspindle and some of the fibers that can be spun. Learning about and using twist energy in ways that only a handspinner can, will introduce unique fabric structures unavailable by any other means. Have fun, and spin a good yarn!

A Romney lamb from Spring Creek Organic Farm, Sandpoint, Idaho.

Ancient Andean spindles

Modern polymer clay spindle

# PROJECTS

## ABBREVIATIONS

K—knit
k2tog—knit 2 sts together
p—purl
pm—place marker
rnd(s)—round(s)
ssk—Slip 2 sts one at a time as if to knit. Insert left needle into these 2 sts from left to right and knit them together.
st(s)—stitch(es)

## General Project Notes

§ **Wraps per inch (w.p.i.):** Measure your yarn by wrapping it snugly around a ruler over one inch and count how many times the yarn wraps around in an inch. The higher the number, the finer the yarn.
Lace = 18 or more w.p.i.
Fingering = 16 w.p.i.
Sport = 14 w.p.i.
Worsted = 12 w.p.i.
Bulky = 10 w.p.i.
Very bulky = 8 or fewer w.p.i.

§ If your commercially prepared fiber seems hard to spin, split it down the middle and then pre-draft sections before you spin.

## PROJECT NOTES:

**Finished size:** 5½ inches from the bottom to the top of the head, 6 inches in diameter around the belly.
**Fiber:** Approximately 2 ounces of angora fiber.
**Yarn:** 3-ply angora yarn about the size of commercial sock yarn. Karen's yarn is denser and has a higher twist than commercial sock yarn. This makes the bag fabric a little more stiff and sturdy than the typical angora knit fabric.
**Gauge:** 11 sts and 16 rows to 2 inches over stockinette.
**Needles:** U.S. size 2 double-pointed needles, crochet hook size D/3.
**Notions:** Stitch markers, red embroidery floss for the eyes, one child's white cotton sock for the lining, approximately ½ cup of uncooked rice for weight.

## Knitted Bunny Bag

*by Karen Pilman*

When I bought my rabbit Calypso in May 2000, I knew the next step was to learn to use her fiber, but I didn't know where to turn. Then in October I happened to stop by a library branch and, lo and behold, there was the local fiber guild's annual exhibit. Thanks to the mentoring of the members of the Greater Birmingham Fiber Guild, I have learned to spin and knit.

Last winter, a member of our guild challenged the rest of us to make a bag, a container of any sort, using any technique and materials that we wanted. At a meeting this past spring we presented our completed bags and explained how they were constructed. The diversity was inspiring and wonderful! I made this bag using Calypso's fur—I tried to capture her quirky character in the bag.

### Gathering the Angora

When I first began gathering my rabbit's fur, I would discard what little soiled fur I found and put everything else—short, long, knots, and all—in a Ziplock bag and compress the air out. Later I found out this was not good for the fibers. Since I have learned to spin and now actually use my fiber, I place the wool in an air-filled bag (without compressing it) or, preferably, in a box where I try to keep the fibers parallel. I have also learned to separate the long fibers (three to five or more inches) and the short fibers (two to three inches).

### Spinning

The angora is so clean that I do not wash it prior to spinning. I have wool carders but they are too coarse for the rabbit fur and cause knots to form. With the angora stored more or less straight there is little need to card.

I spun the yarn for my bunny bag on the Ashford Traditional wheel, but you could also spin this on a handspindle. Since the angora fiber has fewer scales than wool it tends to be silky and slippery. Because of this, I have noticed I need to spin it with more twist.

My three-ply yarn is 100 percent angora, about the size of commercial sock yarn, but much denser in the twist. I spun this yarn early in my spinning experience, so it has too much twist and the bunny bag has yet to fluff because of this. If I were to make another bunny bag, I would spin a two-ply yarn with less twist.

After plying, I washed the spun yarn in shampoo and hot water. I air-dried it for two days, just to make sure it was totally dry before I wound it into a ball.

## THE BUNNY BODY

With the crochet hook, chain 8 sts, slip stitch in first chain to form a ring. With double-pointed needles, pick up and k45 through the crocheted ring. Mark beginning of rnd. Knit in the round in stockinette (k every round) for 3 inches—the first few rounds may be difficult to knit since so many sts will be bunched together.

This sweet bunny bag is made of 100 percent angora, of course! *Spindle courtesy of Linda Diak at Grafton Fibers.*

## SHAPING THE BACK

14 sts are decreased on the bunny back to make the body smaller at the bag opening and the bunny head as follows:

*Decrease rnd 1:* K7, k2tog, place marker (pm), k27, pm, ssk, k7.
*Round 2:* Knit.

Repeat decrease rnd 1 and rnd 2 working decrease over 2 sts before first marker and over 2 sts after second marker until 31 sts remain (14 sts decreased). These decreases will make an inverted "V" on the bunny's back.

## THE BUNNY'S HEAD

After knitting the body, ⅔ of the sts are bound off to make the bag opening and the remaining sts become the head flap as follows:

*Bind off round:* K5, bind off 21 sts, k5.

Transfer remaining 10 sts to one needle. Work back and forth in rows in stockinette for ½ inch.

*Increase row 1:* K in front and back of next st, k to last st, k in front and back of last st (2 sts increased).
*Next row:* Purl.

Repeat last 2 rows twice more (16 sts). K 1 row. P 1 row.

*Decrease row 1:* K5, k2tog, pm, k2tog, pm, ssk, k5.
*Next row:* Purl.

Repeat last 2 rows, decreasing before first marker and after second marker until 4 sts remain. Bind off.

## BUNNY EARS

Leaving a long tail for sewing later, cast on 6 sts. Work back and forth in stockinette for 1¾ inches, then decrease 1 st at the beginning and end of each row until 2 sts remain. Use cast-on tail to sew the ear to top right side of head, just before head increase rows begin. Repeat for second ear, and sew onto top left side of head.

## BUNNY ARMS

Leaving a long tail for sewing later, cast on 4 sts. Knit in stockinette for ¾ inch; bind off. Use cast-on tail to sew on right front body 1½ inches below bind off for bag opening. Sew the arms to the body a second time just above the arm bind off row so they *hang* down. Repeat for second arm, sew onto left front body.

## FINISHING

Make a small pom-pom with angora yarn and sew on rear of bunny for tail. Make a cord by ch 3, sc in first ch to form a ring. Sc in a spiral until cord is 36 inches long.

Attach to inside of bag on either side of opening. To make liner cut two circular pieces from the foot of a child's sock, measuring the circles so they fit inside the bottom of the bag. With right sides together, sew the circular pieces together leaving a 1-inch opening. Turn bag right-side out, fill with rice, and sew opening close (this rice bag gives the bunny bag the weight it needs to stand up). Cut the sock cuff the same height as the bunny bag. Sew the rice bag to one end of the sock cuff. Place the sock bag inside the bunny bag and sew to the opening and bunny neck. Weave in all yarn ends. Sew red bunny eyes on the head using embroidery floss.

Karen used some of her first handspun yarn, spun from Calypso's fur, to make this bag.

# Knitted Handwarmers

TEST DRIVE YOUR HANDSPUN YARN WITH A SWATCH-SIZED PROJECT

*by Mary Spanos*

## PROJECT NOTES:

**Finished size:** Women's medium to large.
**Fiber:** Approximately 1 ounce of a wool and mohair blend roving from Little Barn, Limited.
**Yarn:** Singles, 20 wraps per inch.
**Gauge:** 10 sts and 7 pattern repeats to 2 inches.
**Needles:** U.S. size 3 or size needed to get the correct gauge.
**Note:** These handwarmers are knit flat with the rows going up and down the length of the hand.

These handwarmers are a quick and easy way to *test drive* handspun yarn. They require only a few hours of spinning and knitting and produce a useful swatch that you can admire and contemplate while you complete a bigger project. They also make a great gift!

I dyed the natural colored mohair and wool blend roving with red and fuchsia WashFast acid dyes. When the roving was dry, I tore it in half lengthwise so that I would have two thinner rovings with roughly the same color variations. That way each handwarmer would have the same colors and they would look like a pair.

I predrafted the fiber, wound it loosely around my wrist and started spinning. To spin this slippery and hairy fiber blend, first I spun my spindle to build up some twist. Then I pulled the roving between my hands, letting the fibers slip past each other. When it looked like I had the right amount of fiber for the yarn I wanted to make, I let the twist into the new yarn. Until I have spun for a few yards and evaluated my new yarn, I just have to guess at how much fiber should be in my yarn.

I spun and made yarn until my spindle began to feel heavy. I wound the yarn from the spindle onto a niddy-noddy, removed it from the niddy-noddy, and steamed it to set the twist. I then laid the damp skein over the back of a chair until it dried.

*Horizontal rib pattern*: Knit 2 rows. Purl 2 rows.

Cast on 36 sts or the number of sts needed to reach from the distance 1 inch below your wrist to the knuckle of your little finger. When you cast on leave a 12-inch tail of yarn to use for sewing later. Repeat the horizontal rib pattern until the rectangle measures 7 inches or is long enough to wrap comfortably and snugly around your hand. Bind off leaving a 12-inch tail for sewing. Using the cast on and bind off tails, sew the long edges of the rectangle together, leaving an opening in the middle for your thumb. Make several sts at the thumb edges of the opening to secure the end of the seam.

These handwarmers are actually just a knitted rectangle, about the size of a good swatch that has been sewn into a tube with an opening left for the thumb.

Mary made her own spindle by using a hole cutter and an exotic piece of nicely finished wood from her local specialty hardware store. Handwarmers can be made from just about any warm handspun yarn using many different stitch patterns.

# Crocheted, Felted Hat

*by Amy C. Clarke*

## PROJECT NOTES

**Finished size:** Measurements before felting and after felting:
**From top to brim:** 10 inches (9¼ inches)
**Circumference at brim:** 32 inches (27 inches)
**Diameter across top:** 7 inches (6 inches)
**From top edge to rolled brim:** 5 inches (5 inches)
**Rolled up brim:** 2 inches (2 inches)
**Fiber:** 6 ounces of Bountiful's Alpine Meadow Fibers, "Floral Patchwork" containing a blend of wool, kid mohair, silk, Angelina®, and Holographic Fibers.
**Yarn:** 2-ply yarn measuring 12 wraps per inch
**Gauge:** 10 sts and 10 rows over 2 inches
**Hook:** U.S. size F/5 crochet hook or size needed to get the correct gauge.
**Needle:** Tapestry or yarn needle for sewing in ends
**Note:** You can make this hat using practically any wool except superwash wools that have been chemically treated to prevent felting. Your hat will become fuzzy after it is felted, and fuzzier still if you use a fiber with a higher mohair content (50 percent or more). Use the mini hat sample to determine the necessary hook size if your yarn size is different from what I spun. My hat didn't shrink as much from top to bottom as it did from side to side. Your sample will help you determine where your shrinkage will occur—it may shrink one way more than the other as well.

## ABBREVIATIONS

ch—chain
rnd(s)—round(s)
sc—single crochet
st(s)—stitch(es)
sl st—slip stitch

My favorite felting story occurred when I was in college and doing my laundry at the local Laundromat. It was early in the morning and the place was nearly deserted except for another young woman at the other end of the long line of washers. I had just arrived with my laundry, when I heard her shriek, "Oh! No!" I looked up to see her holding up a baby-sized sweater by the shoulders. Obviously, she didn't mean to transform her favorite cardigan into doll clothes. That was an unfortunate accident. Here's an opportunity to felt on purpose.

### SPINNING

I used a prepared, combed top to spin this yarn. I spun a Z-twist singles yarn that measured about 20 wraps per inch with a fair amount of twist for a sturdy yarn. I also used a woolen spinning technique that allows more air into the yarn as I spun to add loft. I plied the yarn using an S-twist and didn't wash or block it before crocheting.

Spin a lofty, fuzzy yarn to crochet this hat, then plunk the hat in the washer with a load of clothes and felt it!

## SAMPLING

Sampling is absolutely necessary for this project. Crochet a mini hat as the sample. Begin at the top of the hat and make a round, flat disk by ch 3, sc in first ch to form a ring.

*Rnd 1:* Sc 6 sts into the ring.

*Rnd 2:* Sc into sts of first round. Increase frequently at first to keep the disk flat and occasionally as the disk grows to keep the edges from turning up. Increase by working 2 sc into the same st. If your disk starts to bubble, then you increased too much or not enough.

*Remaining rnds:* Continue working sc in spiral and increasing as needed.

When your sample measures 3 inches across, sc 1 rnd without making any increases. **Next rnd:** Decrease by skipping a st about every 6 sts for 1 rnd (or number of sts necessary) to make the edge turn up perpendicular to the top disk to create the sides. Continue working even in sc until the side of the mini hat measures 1 inch, then increase every 4 sts (or the number of sts necessary) for a rnd to make the brim turn up. Sc for 2 or 3 more rnds until the mini hat has a nice little brim (about ½ inch). End with 6 sl sts so that the last rnd blends in with the rnd above and doesn't leave a lump. Fasten off and bury the thread ends.

Spin a Z-twist singles yarn that measures 20 wraps per inch and then ply it S-twist for a plied yarn that measures 12 wraps per inch.

## FELTING THE SAMPLE

Measure your mini hat carefully and write down the measurements. Felt your mini hat by washing it in the washing machine with a load of clothes of a similar color (in case the dyes bleed). Wash it in a hot/cold cycle using a wool-safe detergent. Put it in the dryer with the same load of laundry. Measure your mini hat again and make note of the amount of shrinkage.

## MAKING THE ACTUAL HAT

With this information, you will figure out what percentage the felted sample is compared to the original size so you will know how much bigger to make your actual hat. Do this by dividing the finished sample measurement by the prefelted measurement. That will tell you the percentage of the finished piece compared to the prefelted piece. Then to determine how big to make your hat, divide the desired measurement of the finished hat by that percentage. For example, if the diameter of the sample before felting is 3 inches, and after felting is 2½ inches, the felted piece is 83 percent of the original size: 2.5 inches / 3 inches = .83 (83 percent). If the diameter across the top of your head measures 6 inches, then crochet approximately a 7-inch diameter disk for the top of the hat: 6 inches / .83 = 7.2 inches. Repeat this process for the other measurements.

Measure your head and decide what you want the finished measurements of the hat to be. Follow the instructions for the mini hat but use the new measurements for the top, sides, and brim to make a hat that fits you. Try on your hat frequently as you're working on it to make sure it is too big.

# Woven Scarf

## SPINNING AND WEAVING EXPERIMENTALLY

*by Rosalie Dittmann*

> **PROJECT NOTES:**
>
> **Finished size:** On the loom, the warp measured 10 inches by 70 inches. After I took it off the loom, the scarf measured 8½ inches by 66 inches. After washing, it measured 7 inches by 62 inches.
>
> **Fiber:** Warp and weft is Shropshire-Romney cross wool carded roving and a novelty yarn made from a carded roving of a blend of wool, mohair, and silk dyed orange and red. The finished scarf weighs 3⅜ ounces.
>
> **Yarn:** Approximately 90 yards of the Shropshire-Romney cross yarn spun into a 2-ply yarn that measures 14 wraps per inch. Approximately 53 yards of the novelty yarn spun into a thick and thin novelty 2-ply yarn that measures 15 wraps per inch.
>
> **Sett for scarf:** 6 ends per inch, 6 picks per inch. 57 ends (36 ends of Shropshire-Romney cross, 21 ends of novelty yarn), 90 inches long.
>
> **Pattern for scarf:** 4 harness, plain weave with floats.

For the past year and a half I have made many, many handspun and handwoven scarves. This project started because I just don't like to make samples. So I make scarves instead. I now have twenty-three completed scarves that represent twenty-two different breeds of sheep. The twenty-fourth scarf is on the loom, the twenty-fifth is being spun, and I am waiting for the fiber for scarf number twenty-six, which is on its way from a new friend.

This project began because I had purchased fiber from several members of my guild, The Arachne Spinners in Sturgeon Bay, Wisconsin, who raise animals. My first thought was to pay tribute to these exceptional people and their animals by weaving a scarf of each of their fibers. I finished the first few and brought them to a meeting to see what my friends thought. They gave me great positive feedback and encouraged me to make more. The project grew and grew, becoming more and more exciting.

Spinning and weaving a scarf is a perfect way to sample new fibers, use up bits of leftover fiber or small amounts of novelty yarns and try out new patterns. It requires only several ounces of fiber and it is a quick, small project. There is hardly any loom waste because the tie on, to the front and back beams, becomes the fringe.

## TANYA'S SCARF

The fiber for this yarn came from Tanya King's Shropshire-Romney cross sheep. The orange-red yarn is a blend of wool, mohair, and silk from my stash.

I spun the Shropshire-Romney cross into a fine, even singles, then plied it into a soft two-ply yarn. The novelty blend had thick and thin qualities in its roving form. I was able to enhance this in the spun yarn by pinching and releasing in a rhythmic pattern as I was spinning. Plying it emphasized the thick and thin texture even more. I wanted both yarns to be soft, but strong enough to be used in the warp and weft.

This weave structure looks more complicated than it is. It's fun and easy, and it provides a great way to show off a small amount of precious novelty yarn. I was inspired to design this pattern after seeing Erica De Ruiter's "Child's Bog Jacket" in the Summer 1997 issue of *Weaver's* magazine (pages 56–57). Erica was in turn inspired by the "Prairie Wool Companion's" pattern she saw in the October 1982 *Bogs and Bumps magazine,* (issue 3, pages 18–20). I usually hemstitch at the ends of my scarves, but I found that in this pattern, hemstitching pulled the warp out of alignment. Instead I used Fray Check to stabilize the ends before cutting the scarf from the loom, and then I made a twisted fringe on the ends using 4 ends per group.

I didn't use a floating selvedge as I wove because the pattern at the selvedge is plain weave. However, while

*Rosalie spun two yarns for her scarf—a Shropshire-Romney cross yarn spun into a 2-ply yarn that measures 14 wraps per inch and a blend of wool, mohair, and silk dyed orange and red spun into a thick and thin novelty 2-ply yarn that measures 15 wraps per inch.*

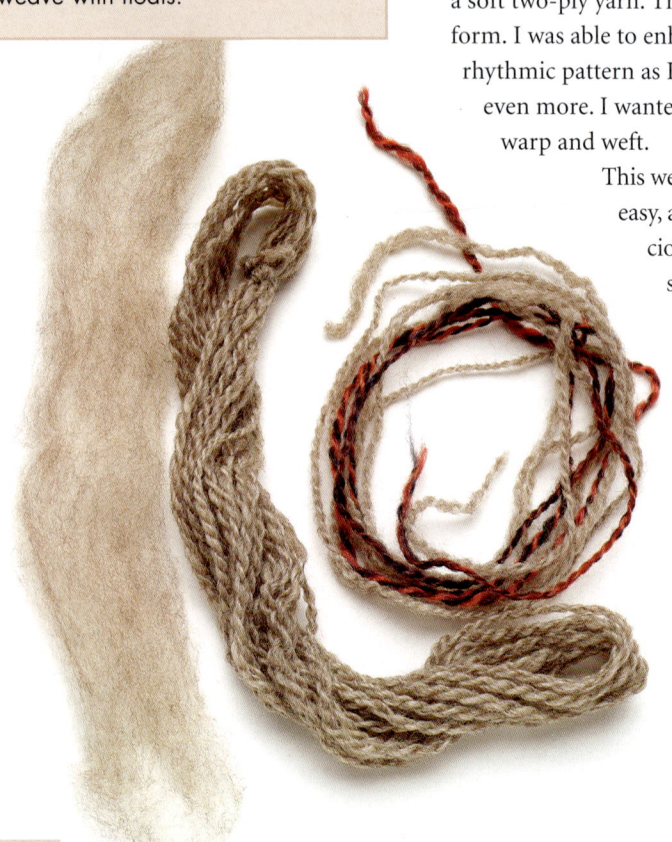

weaving I paid attention to the selvedge edges because when I changed shuttles from the smooth, wool yarn to the novelty yarn, the selvedge tended to bubble out or pull in. In my experience, this bubbling and pulling becomes more noticeable after the garment is washed. I guessed that the Shropshire-Romney yarn would shrink in more because it is 100 percent wool. So as I wove, I applied different tension on it than I did on the blend. I pulled slightly more on the novelty yarn in the float area and slightly less on the wool yarn. I anticipated correctly, and the selvedge was quite straight even after washing.

While weaving, when switching from the wool weft to the novelty weft, I cut the novelty yarn and buried the ends by laying them into the next open shed. Since the novelty is a thick and thin yarn, these ends were not noticeable and I was not dealing with a very long warp length. I decided to cut and bury rather than have the yarn build up at the selvedge edge as it would if I had hidden the warp floats in the selvedge edge.

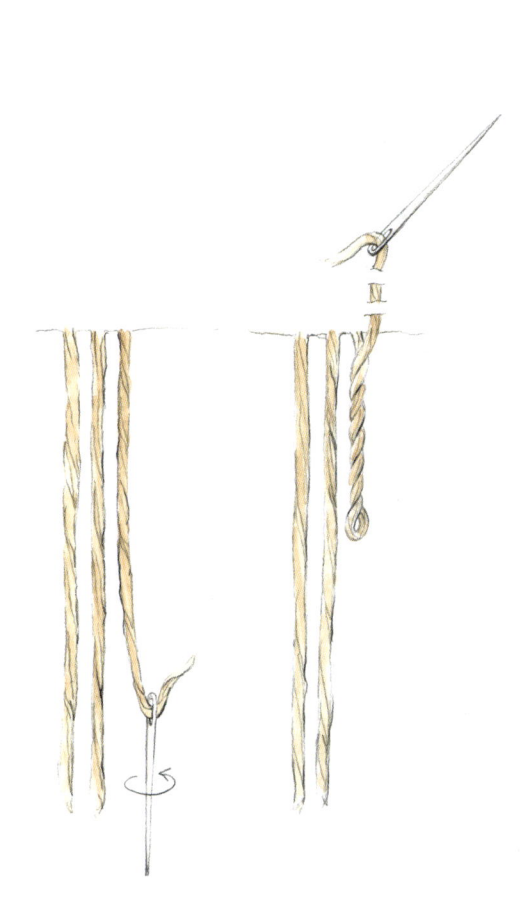

making twisted fringe

Rosalie Dittmann wanted to try out the various types bers of her guild who raise fiber animals. She start each fleece she bought—so far she's made 26 sc works!

## PROJECT NOTES:

**Finished Size:** 14 by 9 inches

**Fiber:** 2 ounces of space-dyed wool roving

**Needles:** Two U.S. size 5 double-pointed knitting needles, tapestry needle

**Yarn:** 2-ply yarn that measures 10 wraps per inch

**Gauge:** 12 stitches and 18 rows to 2 inches over pattern

# Knitted Turquoise Tornado Baby Cap

*by Dustin Wedekind*

This little baby hat is an easy way to use up odd bits of fluff—its height is determined by how much yarn you have.

Spinning with dyed roving is very fun. The multiple colors seem random, yet they go together so nicely. It is exciting to watch the colors change through the process—from the bright splotches of roving, to the thin lines on a bobbin, to the shifting colors of the plied yarn, and finally into patterns in a woven or knitted garment. In an effort to keep the color closer to gradations in the roving, this hat is knitted in a narrow strip—that means the yarn passes back and forth in a shorter distance, keeping the color together longer resulting in smoother gradations of color.

*Step 1:* Cast on 12 sts leaving a 12-inch long tail. * Knit three rows. Purl three rows. Repeat from * for about 60 inches. Bind off.

*Step 2:* Use the tapestry needle and the tail to join the side edges together at the point that the hat will fit around the wearer's head (*Figure 1*). Match purl rows to knit rows like a checkerboard. Stitch together for about 4 inches.

*Figure 1*

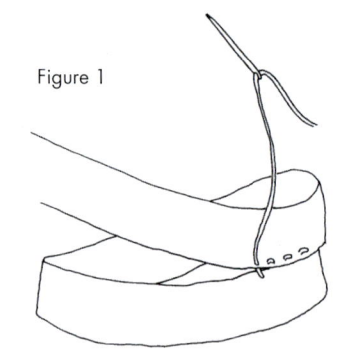

*Step 3:* When you are half-way around the first coil, begin to stitch two sts in from the edge under the upper coil and continue stitching along the edge of the bottom coil (*Figure 2*). This will cause the upper coil to overlap the lower coil, creating a lip. Match the purl rows to the knit rows for at least one turn around the hat.

*Figure 2*

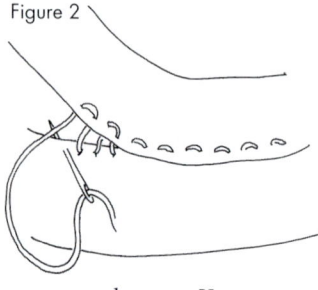

*Step 4:* To begin forming the cone shape, go through two sts of the bottom coil every third stitch to create a decrease. You may decrease more often to close the hat up, or decrease fewer times to make a longer hat. After a few rounds of stitching, you will see how quickly you need to decrease. It is a bit of a guessing game, but it is easy to re-do the joining sts if you need to change the frequency of decrease sts.

*Step 5:* When you reach the end of the coil, stitch the bound edge to the edge of the coil.

...mall bits of leftover fiber to spin the yarn for this baby hat.
... strips that he sewed into a spiraling cone.